Aesthetics at work

Arne Melberg (ed.)

Unipub forlag 2007

ISBN 978-82-7477-294-6

This book has been produced with economical support from the project
Aesthetics at work, financed by the Norwegian Research Council

Publisher:
Unipub AS, Oslo 2007

Printed in Norway:
AiT e-dit AS, Oslo 2007

Content

Introduction

This anthology is the result of a research project that ran from 2004 to 2006 at the University of Oslo, financed by the Norwegian Research Council. The participants came from different departments – literature, music, art and media – but worked together in their investigations of *aesthetics at work*. The focus has been on aesthetic processes in contemporary culture, on the historical, theoretical and technological premises for these processes, and on the trends in these processes, which we sum up in terms of *aestheticisation*. We had research partners and contributors from Stockholm, Copenhagen, Frankfurt and New York. One of the results of the work with our research partners was a conference entitled *The Relevance of the Aesthetic*, held in June 2006. A written report from this conference can be found on the website of the project: www.hf.uio.no/estetikk (go to Arkiv).

This is how we presented the project in our application:

> Under the heading Aesthetics at work we propose a project for basic research on the changing state of the arts and the incorporation and relevance of the aesthetic dimension in daily life in general. The research will deal with the historical and contemporary development of the media, technology, institutions, economy and philosophy of the arts. Studies will not be restricted to the arts, however, but the emphasis will be given to aesthetics at work: the arts in their interaction, new aesthetical forms (including the new techniques of the information industry), new aesthetical activities, media and expressions including aesthetical dimensions in current economical and technological development, all those aesthetical tendencies that contribute to our world today.
>
> The focus of the research will therefore be on the arts, with an emphasis on new forms of art, on aesthetic theory and on the processes of aestheticisation, in order to grasp profound changes of art and aesthetics in contemporary social and economical life.
>
> Our proposal has a simple basis, observed by many and of obvious importance for us all: the diminishing importance of the arts in their traditional forms in relation to the increasing importance of aesthetical dimensions in new fields of social life and interaction, not least within

> the economical sphere. The arts have traditionally been represented by works of art and the philosophy and criticism of art and aesthetics have likewise been based upon the work of art. The work of art is certainly not obsolete but has a prolific life in the institutions of art. The impression of a diminishing importance of the arts has not to do with the disappearance of the object but with the dramatic expansion of new fields of expression. The most important changes come from the work of aesthetics within types of activities that are either new or not bound to the work of art. The industry of advertising is an obvious example, but there are many more: journalism, specially feature-journalism and copy-writing, dramatised and scenographic arrangements of everything from news to accounts to clothes to homes, cooking (including the activity itself and the presentation of food), music arranged for and in shops, lifts, airport-"showers", music enormously expanding as an industry with new forms for production and reproduction, museums changing from object-gathering to experience-producing, production (also in the economical sense) of virtual experience rather than objects, "culture" as an important reason for settlement as well as for tourism, an aesthetic development of the sports, private life itself (and not least sex life) becoming more public and in that process given an aesthetical dimension.
>
> The reasons for these on-going transformations are of course manifold but can be summarised in terms of media (media in a wide and differentiated sense, including all kinds of information and communication), institutions (including the traditional institutions of art but apparently also old and new social institutions being invaded by aesthetics), technology (including new forms and devices for the production of communication and the democratisation of their use), economy (as the development of a cultural field of economical importance). These vehicles combine to develop a field of aesthetics that goes far beyond the traditional field that was primarily based on the work of art. It is our ambition to develop a united effort to grasp this new field of research.

The essays collected in this volume investigate different aspects of the vast area described above and we hope that they thereby provide a general picture of the status of the field of aesthetics today – aesthetics in theory as well as aesthetics at work in the arts and in real life – and we hope thereby to demonstrate and analyse the tendency of aestheticisation. *Arnfinn Bø-Rygg*, faculty professor of aesthetics, outlines current trends in the theory of aesthetics and the growing interest in somatic and atmospheric aspects of aesthetics in this theory; *Liv Hausken*, associate professor in media studies, examines the technical and socio-cultural conditions for the aesthetics of x-ray imaging; *Ina Blom*, associate professor in art history, discusses the relationship between light and lamps in modern art and the articulation and production of social sites in an environmental aesthetics;

Synne Skjulstad, PhD.student in intermedia, studies the conflicts between usability and aesthetics in web design and the potential resolution of these conflicts in communicational aesthetics; *Tellef Kvifte*, professor in musicology, discusses the relationship between digital and analogue techniques in musical sampling, showing how closely these techniques are interrelated, and thereby also showing their implications for cultural theory; *Marius Wulfsberg*, PhD in comparative literature, gives a series of examples of changing interrelations between the photographic image and the literary text, thereby demonstrating cultural changes in concepts of fiction and attitudes to reality; and *Arne Melberg*, professor of comparative literature, outlines a theory of prose, indicating prosification as an aspect of the tendency of aestheticisation, and examines some examples from the front-line of literary prose.

Arnfinn Bø-Rygg:

"Sunday in Breadth"

Aesthetics as a field and subject

I

The current relevance of aesthetics

Aesthetics is on a roll. Some people are talking of "the aesthetic turn", on the analogy of "the linguistic turn" in philosophy that was established in the 1960s. A mere look at the aesthetics anthologies, histories of aesthetics and aesthetics encyclopedias that have been published in the past fifteen years will confirm the considerable current interest in aesthetics. The aesthetics anthologies (particularly Anglo-American) are so numerous that there is no point in listing them or highlighting some to the detriment of others. Every self-respecting publishing house has its "textbook" containing classic texts (and recent comments). The same also largely applies to histories of aesthetics and encyclopedias.[1]

The interest in aesthetics bears witness to movement and change – some would say a crisis – in the field of aesthetics and in the subject of aesthetics. It is not difficult to find reasons for this. I think they can be divided into four groups: 1) The art world's own engagement in (aesthetic) theory; 2) increased awareness of the significance of aesthetic reflection in aesthetic subjects; 3) the emphasis on 'aesthetic experience' in various types of aesthetics; 4) extension of the concept of aesthetics.

Among other things the art world's awareness of theory may be viewed as a result of lines of development in art, and the most extreme

[1] Cf. E. Souriau ed.: *Vocabulaire d'esthétique*, PUF, Paris 1990; M. Kelley ed.: *Encyclopedia of Aesthetics*, four volumes, Oxford University Press, 1998; K.Marck et al. ed.: *Ästhetische Grundbegreiffe*, six volumes, Meltzer Verlag, Stuttgart, 2000-2006.

conception of this would be a variant of Hegel's theory of "the end of art": When one can no longer see the difference between a work of art and a pure and simple thing (Warhol's soup can and a soup can in a grocery store), the aesthetic difference is not a visual or sensory difference (Danto's "indiscernibility" thesis). It is "an atmosphere of theory" that makes Warhol's soup can art. Thus, art has realized its own determination, and further development can only take place as art's own philosophy. However the art world's own theoretical awareness reaches further and follows paths other than this example (and interpretation of it) shows. Even at the beginning of the 1960s the composer Pierre Boulez talked about the necessity of an *orientation esthétique* in artistic practice, and since then many important artists have followed this up.

The increased awareness of the significance of aesthetic reflection in aesthetic subjects is demonstrated by the fact that humanistic subjects such as art history, musicology, literary theory, theatre and media studies are called "aesthetic subjects" at all, so that when we use this designation we are not homing in on practical-aesthetic subjects. For example, the Norwegian Research Council's programme "Fundamental problems in aesthetic research" (1989–93) was the expression of such a reorientation, an interest in what is common to these subjects, "the fundamental aesthetic problems".[2] The scepticism of neo-rhetoric and philosophy or their rejection of aesthetics was a bygone stage.

The focus on 'aesthetic experience' has been demonstrated by the breakthrough that phenomenologically oriented aesthetics has seen, as well as the rebirth of Dewey's pragmatic aesthetics. In particular a large part of the post-war period's analytically oriented aesthetics, that in many ways was a "meta-aesthetics", was characterized by dryness and "dreariness" (Passmore), that often left it empty of experience. This was in strong contrast to the two inspirers of this aesthetics: Beardsley and Wittgenstein; Beardsley, who always took examples and based his conclusions on experience, and Wittgenstein, who freely disseminated aesthetic judgments, all the way down to the idiosyncratic ones. Perhaps this was the meta-aesthetics the American painter Barnett Newman was thinking about, when he said that

[2] Cf. Series of publications EST. Fundamental problems in aesthetic research, 1-12, The Norwegian Research Council (Norges allmennvitenskapelige forskningsråd) 1991-1996.

"Aesthetics is for artists what ornithology is for birds." – In Germany the research group "Poetik und Hermeneutik"[3] and the "Kolloquium Kunst und Philosophie"[4] were criticizing traditional aesthetics as an "Ästhetik von oben", empty of experience. It would not be incorrect to say that the aesthetics which declares that it wishes to be pure *aesthetics* and nothing more is the most general and abstract one. At times it has had the same character as Kierkegaard accused epistemology of having, when he compared this to inviting a person to dinner and only serving him the menu card.

Extension of the concept of aesthetics has gone in different directions, but all of them have their point of departure in the aesthetics term's Greek origin, *aisthesis* (sense perception). The later Foucault talked of an "aesthetics of existence", a creation of oneself and formation of one's own life he believed he could see in Baudelaire's dandyism, but also in the ancient Greeks' occupation with dietary questions (cf. Gr. *diaita* = mode of life) as part of an ethical practice. Richard Shusterman goes further in focusing on the body in his "somaesthetics" (cf. Gr. soma = body)[5]. Naturally, "environmental aesthetics", which was launched at the beginning of the 1980s, belongs to extension of the areas of the aesthetic, and is of importance to planners, architects and designers. Work on ecological aesthetics belongs here (Gernot Böhme). I will examine Schusterman and Böhme more closely later in the article.

Criticism of aesthetics

Nevertheless criticism of aesthetics is strong and it comes from various sources. For some people "the return to the aesthetic" was a conservative move with corresponding values. Practically a classic in that connection is Hal Foster's *The Anti-Aesthetic. Essays on Postmodern Culture*, from 1983. Foster identifies "the aesthetic" with a privileged aesthetic area and concepts such as (a special) 'aesthetic experience' and 'taste'. Contrary to this the anti-aesthetic postmodern theory of culture is cross-disciplinary and open to cultural forms

---

[3] This work resulted in a number of voluminous publications where leading literary experts such as Hans Robert Jauss, Wolfgang Iser, Karlheinz Stierle, philosophers such as Reinhart Koselleck, Manfred Frank, Odo Marquard, art historians such as Max Imdahl and Gottfried Boehm, and music experts such as Carl Dahlhaus took part.

[4] See for example Gottfried Boehm's article "Kunsterfahrung als Herausforderung der Ästhetik" in volume 1 of this series.

[5] *The Journal of Aesthetics and Art Criticism* 57:3, summer 1999.

that are politically engaged or rooted in everyday life (Foster 1983, p. XV). Foster does not attempt to reinterpret or transform aesthetic concepts, nor does he therefore see that concepts and categories from the history of aesthetics throw light on or even have characteristics in common with today's theory of culture. In *The Ideology of the Aesthetic* (1990) Terry Eagleton remarks that early aesthetics was occupied with the body and perception, but that it was soon colonized by reason (p. 15). His procedure of ideological criticism is far too superficial regarding the independence and abundance of the aesthetic tradition. The fact that Eagleton without more ado subscribes to Hegel's criticism of Kant shows that he is far from updated concerning the area. Even less updated is the group in England calling itself "new Philistines" in its attack on the new upgrading of aesthetics, which it views as elitistic. What is labelled as "new aestheticism", is a far distance from aestheticism in the traditional sense.[6] – In *L'Art de l'âge moderne* (1992) and *Adieu à l'esthétique* (2000) Jean-Marie Schaeffer accuses aesthetics of being empty, speculative metaphysics. In his view even Nietzsche cannot free himself from the speculative theory of culture. It consecrates the work of art and does not distinguish between evaluation and description. With the exception of what he views as an unfinished project by Kant, what he calls his "meta-aesthetics", Schaeffer rejects aesthetics as unusable (Schaeffer pp. 55–64).[7]

While some people accuse aesthetics of having deprived art of its power, others of consecrating art, one leading art philosopher of our time, Arthur Danto, maintains that "aesthetic considerations have no essential applications to what I shall speak of as "art after the end of art" – i.e., art produced from the 1960s on" (Danto 1997, p. 25). It is an atmosphere of theory which makes an object a work of art. This undergoes a transfiguration, as it says in his most important book, *The Transfiguration of the Commonplace* (Danto 1981). You could say that transfiguration plays the same role in his understanding of readymades in terms of art philosophy as transubstantiation does in theology. Danto's prime example is Warhol's *Brillo Box.* According to Danto this work of art is not markedly different

[6] Cf. D. Beech and J. Roberts (eds), *The Philistine Controversy*, London: Verso, 2002, which contains among other things the original discussion in *New Left Review*, Nos 218 and 225.

[7] Besides Schaffer's books, cf. No. 414 of *Magazine littéraire*, November 2002, which is entitled "Philosophie & Art. La fin de l'esthétique?".

from Brillo boxes in the supermarket and makes it clear that one cannot distinguish art from reality on a perceptual basis. Thus it is non-aesthetic. Correspondingly Danto only sees *artistic* qualities in Duchamp's *Fountain,* not aesthetic ones (perceptual or affective). He quotes Duchamp as having the same view: "Aesthetic delectation is the danger to be avoided" and "This choice (i.e. of readymades) was based on a reaction of visual indifference with at the same time a total absence of good or bad taste... in fact a complete anaesthesis". Danto further rejects beauty as necessary for art and for the definition of art, something which does not mean that beauty is a relevant criterion in earlier art. Beauty is quite simply an outdated Hegelian concept. All in all Danto's concept of aesthetics is narrow since he identifies the aesthetic dimension with perceptible formal qualities, perceptual pleasure, beauty. It is from this that the sharp distinction he wishes to make between the philosophy of art and aesthetics is derived. Thus Danto ignores *the reflexive dimension* as a topos in aesthetics from its beginning (see below).

However, a certain movement and change can be detected in Danto's latest book, *The Abuse of Beauty: Aesthetics and the Concept of Art* (2003). In the foreword Danto talks cautiously of the work of art's "pragmatic" qualities, "inflectors" which "colour" the meaning contained in the work of art. This is as far as Danto will go in the direction of acknowledging aesthetic aspects in contemporary works of art. In his ForArt lecture 2005 he says that "it would be a major transformation in artistic practice if artists were to begin making art, the point and purpose of which was aesthetic experience. That would be a revolution" (Danto 2005 p 14). At the same time he paves the way for what he calls a deeper concept of aesthetics, which he attributes to Charles Sanders Peirce, who utilized three normative disciplines – logic, ethics and aesthetics – where aesthetics was the most fundamental one. Danto quotes Peirce from his Lecture 5, where it is quite apparent that by the aesthetic dimension Peirce is indicating a broad category of what is aesthetically "good". "There is no such thing as positive aesthetic badness.... All there will be will be various aesthetic qualities". Peirce links these to moods, which Danto thinks approaches what Heidegger understood by Dasein's Stimmungen, i.e. modes that characterize the state of existence. Danto says: "I think terror, as exploited by the Department of Homeland Security is a *Stimmung* – a mood in which everything is disclosed as threatening" (ibid. p 16).

I shall go on with this a little, because it will be a crucial point later in the article. Danto concludes his section on Pierce by saying that he admires Peirce and Heidegger because they

> have sought to liberate aesthetics from its traditional preoccupation with beauty, and beauty's traditional limitation to calm detachment – and at the same time to situate the beauty as part of the ontology of being human. But this would be the mood we are put into by beautiful days or beautiful settings (ibid. p. 17).

Thus beauty is for Danto something that belongs to life, not necessarily to art and aesthetics. Nevertheless, some contemporary works of art have beauty as one of their features, like for example Maya Lin's *Viet Nam Veterans' Memorial.* In a reply to his critics in connection with a symposium on *The Abuse of Beauty* he says that

> The Vietnam Veterans' Memorial uses beauty because beauty heals, and the purpose of the monument was "to heal a nation", which it really helped do. But it provided a site in which viewers will meditate on war, death, loss and beauty long after the war that occasioned it has subsided into history. It really does what Hegel says that art once did – it satisfies the highest needs of the spirit (p 200). [8]

It is stated in *The Abuse of Beauty*, where this example is also taken, that in such a work Danto finds *internal* beauty. It is intended; we understand beauty as a result of the fact that we have understood the meaningful content. However, beauty is necessary for life, not for art, and for Danto the aesthetic primarily concerns our life-world. In a polemic exchange at the conference "Rediscovering Aesthetics", at University College Cork, Ireland, in the summer of 2004, Danto draws an experience from 9/11 into this life-world:[9]

> What really got me started in aesthetics at all – not as an academic discipline, but as a living thing – were the shrines that were set up all over New York City the day after 9/11. They were put together spontaneously out of balloons, cards, and flowers. No one taught anyone how to do that, or gave anyone instructions for how to put them on the sidewalk, in foyers, in stairways. I wondered why people responded not with anger but with beauty. No artist could have done better. That phenomenon does raise the question of where beauty fits in the normal, or abnormal, course of human life (Elkins 2006 p 71).

---

[8] *Inquiry* Vol. 48, No.2, April 2005, pp. 189-200.

[9] In J. Elkins (ed.), *Art History Versus Aesthetics*, Routledge, London 2006.

Thus Danto here utilizes a broad or extended concept of aesthetics, in line with many in the contemporary discussion of aesthetics. However, his re-use of the aesthetics concept does not involve any necessary especially interesting connection between art and aesthetics, art and beauty. In that sense he still has a narrow concept of aesthetics, which is atypical in today's discussion. Furthermore, he has a narrow concept of beauty, where there is neither room for Baudelaire's "modern beauty", Rilke's "frightful beauty", Schönberg's dissonances (of which the composer said that "my music is not beautiful"), or that beauty which according to Benjamin burns up, like a veil.

II

Aesthetics as a problem

In a large part of the history of aesthetics the concept of aesthetics has been a problem. For Kant the concept was a problem, likewise for Hegel, two of the most central figures in the history of aesthetics. Kant maintained that Baumgarten had made philosophy unclear with his aesthetics concept and distinguished between aesthetics as a theory of a priori sensibility and aesthetics as experience of the beautiful and the sublime. Hegel's aesthetics apply to "the philosophy of beautiful art", and he only accepted the term "aesthetics" because it had entered into linguistic usage. Things did not get better in the 20th century. Heidegger wished to "conquer" aesthetics, which he regarded as a part of traditional metaphysics (from Plato to Nietzsche). For Wittgenstein aesthetics' questions and answers were "totally misunderstood". A third central thinker in the past century, Adorno, opens his "early introduction" to *Aesthetic Theory* with the following statement: "The concept of philosophical aesthetics has an antiquated quality, as does the concept of a system or that of morals" (Adorno 1997, p 332). According to himself, Adorno's *Aesthetic Theory* was intended to discount Friedrich Schlegel's statement: "What is called the philosophy of art usually lacks one of two things: either the philosophy or the art". (p 366). For Adorno art and the aesthetic experience always held a central position. However, for Martin Heidegger and Ludwig Wittgenstein too the question of the nature of art was of crucial importance to their thinking. This is in spite of the fact that neither of them actually has any "aesthetics". Today we would nevertheless say that both Wittgenstein and

Heidegger, and for that matter both Foucault and Deleuze, have an aesthetic philosophy or an aesthetic thinking. Roland Barthes may be typical for what has taken place. He too had an ingrown scepticism to the term 'aesthetic'. However, in *Roland Barthes par Roland Barthes* he designates precisely his own discourse as "aesthetic":

> He attempts to compose a discourse which is not uttered in the name of the Law and/or of Violence: whose instance might be neither political nor religious nor scientific; which might be in a sense the remainder and the supplement of all such utterances. What shall we call such discourse? *Erotic*, no doubt, for it has to do with pleasure; or even perhaps: *aesthetic*, if we foresee subjecting this old category to a gradual torsion which will alienate it from its regressive, idealist background and bring it closer to the body, to the *drift*. (Barthes 1977, p. 84).

It is precisely such a "torsion" of the aesthetics concept that has taken place since Barthes wrote this (1974). Barthes' suggestion then, is in line with developments within aesthetics in the past 20 years. Aesthetics is not merely the theory of beauty, but applies to the senses, to sensory experience. The later Barthes' aesthetic discourse is a discourse where bodily sensations are given expression, as a form of knowledge. It is a matter of registering precise and individual experience in each and every case. To a high degree Barthes thinks aesthetically; he has an aesthetic thinking, both in a narrow and a broad sense: Art has a central position, but not least the perceptual and perceived experience.

However, resistance to the concept of aesthetics has been considerable. Jacques Rancière would claim that aesthetics comes into existence as its name is rejected.[10] Rancière is of the opinion that even if Baumgarten invented the name "aesthetics", it did not start with him; Baumgarten has a "generalized poetics" (Osborne 2000, p. 19), something which makes aesthetics an impossibility, since it replaces poetics. Rancière regards poetics and aesthetics as two different modes of thought. In other words he allots aesthetics great, not to mention fundamental, significance, like others who stand for an extension of the concept of aesthetics.

---

[10] Cf. "What aesthetics can mean", in: Peter Osborne (ed), *From an Aesthetic Point of View. Philosophy, Art and the Senses*, Serpent's Tail, London 2000, p 18.

The extended concept of aesthetics

The person who has most systematically developed an extended concept of aesthetics is Wolfgang Welsch. Welsch wishes to include the current forms of aestheticisation (Welsch 1997). With him this concept (and the phenomena) are not only negatively charged. He distinguishes between a superficial aestheticisation (catchwords: beautification, animation, community of experience) and in-depth aestheticisation; the latter applies to the condition of the material world, the social dimension, the individual-subjective dimension and in the final concerns our conception of reality. The basic thesis is that if the epistemological theory of bases or foundations remains credible, then it must be aesthetically or *aisthetically* impregnated. And the conditions of our world are such that they require an aesthetic style of thinking. We live in an aesthetic paradigm. Welsch wishes to have an aesthetics which opens out towards the whole extent of *aisthesis*, an *aisthetics* in contrast to aesthetics or *artistics.* Aesthetics became artistics from and including Hegel.

However Welsch goes further. He wishes to show that the aestheticisation of epistemology already begins with Baumgarten and Kant, has Nietzsche as a representative in the 19th century (reasonably enough) and that both Wittgenstein and Rorty are representatives of the aestheticisation process in the 20th century. It is Kant in the first critique Welsch refers to here, the transcendental aesthetics concerning the a priori conditions of sensibility, the forms of intuition. Welsch sums up his survey in the following way:

> In the past two hundred years truth, knowledge and reality have progressively taken on aesthetic contours. First of all it has proved to be the case that aesthetic components are fundamental to our awareness and our reality. It began with Kant's transcendental aesthetics and stretches on to the self-reflection of the natural sciences in our time. Secondly, that insight demonstrated successively that the properties of cognition and reality are aesthetic. It was Nietzsche's discovery, which also since then, primarily by enlisting nautical metaphors was given expression by others and reaches further on to the constructivism of our time. Reality is not a fixed existing element independent of understanding, but the object of a construction (Welsch 1996, p 52).

I shall not comment in detail on Welsch concerning this point, other than firstly to point out that his "epistemological aestheticisation" is far too great a tale. Moreover: Naturally we can say that each determined form of reality is a construction of our cognition. But this applies to something *determined as* real, our view of this reality, the object of our cognition, but a reality as produced by us. The reason that Welsch can claim that he is not developing a new fundationalism with aesthetics or aisthetics as a basis, is that the fundamental *aesthetic* nature of reality and thinking in his view abjures such fundationalism. Aesthetic thinking is a universal form of thinking and a primary philosophy, Welsch would say, but not in a traditional sense.

With astonishingly good, old-fashioned German thoroughness and systematism Welsch has developed his aestheticisation thesis, where he distinguishes among other things between nine different applications or aspects of the aesthetic dimension.[11] Despite different meanings of 'aestheticisation' Weslsch finds a sufficient family likeness between them to make the concept applicable. Correspondingly he conducts an analysis of the concept of 'the aesthetic factor' and differentiates and clarifies its many dimensions: sensory, perceptual, semantic, hedonistic, subjective, conciliatory, cosmetic, uplifting, artistic, callistic, sensitive and virtual. These are then placed in three primary fields of significance: sensibility, perception (the *aesthetic element)*; art (the *artistic element*); beauty (the *callistic-sublime element*). The multiplicity of meanings makes it possible, according to Welsch, to evaluate the phenomenon of aestheticisation in a complex way. Rather than denying or affirming the phenomenon, the deeper aspects of aestheticisation must be accepted as unavoidable, whereas there are many reasons for criticism of aestheticisation's superficial phenomena. However, acceptance of the situation is a condition of criticism. To an increasing degree reality is aesthetically constructed. This demands a new type of *aesthetic thinking* which is on a level with the situation. In this connection Welsch accepts "distraction" (Benjamin), a form of reception based on free-flowing attention and habit. Aesthetic thinking is distracted aisthetic perception, interpretation and reflection. It accepts plurality, sharpens the awareness of dispute (Lyotard) and sensibilizes recognition of the an-aesthetic, the reverse side of the aesthetic.

Like Welsch Gernot Böhme utilizes the expression "aisthetics" or "the new aesthetics" which is understood as a general theory of perception.[12] This aesthetics stands in contrast to art and judgement aesthetics. Its point of departure is that we are currently dealing with an

---

[11] W. Welsch 1997.

[12] G. Böhme, *Aisthetik. Vorlesungen über Ästhetik als allgemeine Wahrnehmungslehre*, W. Fink Verlag, Munich 2001.

extended aesthetic production, or extended aesthetic work, which has aesthetic value or presentational value (in addition to use value and exchange value). Aesthetic production is concerned with presentation or staging of goods, cities, landscapes etc., where *design* becomes the central element not only of industrial production but of town planning, advertising, acoustics and even the self-perception of human beings. Like Welsch Böhme also uses 'aestheticisation' as a positive concept. However the fundamental concept of the new, extended aesthetics is, according to Böhme, '*atmosphere*', which recently has been given broad prominence in the discussion of architecture. Böhme defines atmosphere as "spaces, in that they are "thinged" by the presence of objects, of human beings or environmental constellations, i.e. through the ecstasies of these. They are themselves spheres of the presence of something, its reality in space" (Böhme 1995). Böhme talks of production of atmospheres. I shall comment briefly on this. To my opinion atmosphere could be a fruitful concept.[13]

'Atmosphere' originally means the layer of air that surrounds the earth.[14] In this way it also means the air one is surrounded by and breathes in. We could say that a place has an atmosphere and time has its atmosphere. Goethe's literary works (which were indivisible from his meteorological observations and speculations), Schubert's bugle calls (which suggest distance, a place of remembrance) and impressionistic art and music are strongly characterized by the atmospheric. The danger with the concept of atmosphere is that it may become too tame or too mild. However, it does not have to be that way. György Ligeti had a very good reason for calling one of his transitional compositions (around 1960) "Atmosphères". In this piece Ligeti detaches himself from traditional types of formal structure and develops a static form of music or more correctly: a tonal texture that develops continually and whose internal structure is exceedingly complex. Another mode of listening is required: The listener experiences a motionless tapestry of sound that changes in tonal colour. He must eschew structural listening (the modernistic ideal), because the method of composition deviates from the structural, to be more precise the serial, which according to Ligeti at that

---

[13] G. Böhme, *Atmosphäre. Essays zur neuen Ästhetik*, Suhrkamp, Frankfurt am M., 1995.

[14] From neo-Latin 'atmosphaera', which stems from Greek 'atmos', vapour and 'sphaira', globe.

time had evolved to a point where the fully determined was transformed into the completely random.

The concept of atmosphere refers to our place in what Heidegger calls 'the dimension' – between earth and heaven. It has the quite concrete meaning of following the changes in the seasons, being subject to the weather, climate, light and shade. Architects such as Frank Lloyd Wright have taken this into consideration in a decisive manner: the meaning of air, the interplay between air and water. One advantage of the concept of atmosphere is that it is vague. It may be too vague, stand as another word for "Je ne sais quoi" – this "I don't know what" – which early aesthetics assigned to art or beauty. However it does not have to be meaningless, but precisely an expression of the undetermined, the difficult or unspeakable, the mysterious, or what is – as Adorno said – "more" regarding works of art or nature. The concept is fruitful if it is not absolutized, as Böhme has a tendency to do, but is used in constellation with other concepts. The advantages are many. In addition to those I have mentioned: It is a typical "intermediate" concept, between subject and object, and avoids both the temptations of subjectivism and objectivism. It is less subjectivist than mood and less objectivist than the concept of "character" (Sedlmayr, Norberg-Schulz). The obvious thing about the concept of atmosphere is its natural-aesthetic context, or perhaps the ecological foundation that Böhme assigns to it. It is a phenomenological concept par excellence, and refers to our world of experience, the concrete perceived world we live in, where the sun rises in the east and sets in the west, i.e. not the world of science. If we say that what we might roughly call phenomenological aesthetics (Heidegger, Merleau-Ponty, Lyotard, the later Barthes) works with a continuum of sensation – imagination – symbolization, then it is clear that the concept of atmosphere is located at the level of sensation. However, not so much perception as the holistic, undifferentiated being sensible of, breathing-in[15]. The concept of atmosphere must retain its vagueness. A catalogue for producing atmospheres cannot be issued. Nor can they be deduced from elements or archetypes. Construction of atmospheres may easily be a restraint in

[15] In the Encyclopedia of Aesthetics, Vol. 3, David Summers writes informatively about the origin of the word aesthesis: "Aisthesis descends from a word meaning "to breathe", an archaic metaphor for perception as pneumatic. ... Things, as it were, breathe themselves out, we, as it were, breathe them in, and on this etymological view aesthesis is of a piece with life itself" (p. 428).

architecture and urban environments. The secretion of certain scents would be an annoyance if they were part of the built environment.[16] Probably the conscious use of the effects of atmospheres is best suited to the theatre stage, which is often carefully planned.

Since the 1980s the concept of 'environmental aesthetics' has come into play (Carlson 1982, Berleant 1992) within Anglo-American aesthetics. Its development corresponds to the awareness of the significance of the environment for us as sensory beings, the significance of contexts, the significance of nature and our dependence on and interaction with it. Environmental aesthetics is of course not new. It gives new relevance to natural aesthetics which Hegel and Croce had driven out of aesthetics, but which characteristically enough Adorno wished to rehabilitate.

Another extension of the aesthetic is taking place within the pragmatic tradition, with Richard Shusterman's *somaesthetics.* Within the Anglo-American tradition somaesthetics is critical of parts of analytical aesthetics, which Shusterman thinks have led to an an-aestheticisation of aesthetics and art (Danto). Shusterman grasps the meaning of aesthetics as the thematization of the corporeal dimension of sensibility and perception. In the programmatic article "Somaesthetics: A Disciplinary Proposal" (Shusterman 2000) he points out that since Baumgarten the corporeal dimension has been implicit in aesthetics through its emphasis on sensibility and sensuality. Aesthetics for Baumgarten is not merely a thematization of the sensory, but has to do with perfection of the sensory expression, i.e. an improvement or refinement of the sensory capacity for knowledge. Thus, Shusterman finds in Baumgarten a practical aesthetic programme which aims at improvements in our capacities for perception, something which later aesthetics forgot. Shusterman wishes to revive this "meliorative" and pragmatic aspect of aesthetics, i.e. view aesthetics as "a discipline for perfecting perception and thus action". Shusterman could have referred to John Cage and his art in this, Cage who wishes to sharpen and improve *aesthesis* through his disciplined implementation of sound.

Shusterman's somaesthetics is to be regarded as a discipline in both senses of the word: "as a branch of learning or instruction" and

---

[16] It appears different with what grows forth. H.P. L'Orange has provided an unforgettable description of the atmosphere in a Roman street, where he uses words such as "airing", "spirit", "emanation", "vapour", "cosmic balsam". Cf. H.P. L'Orange 1971, p. 124.

"as a corporal form of training or exercise". Thus it shall be partly a corporeal field of research, partly a corporeal discipline, i.e. the performance itself of corporeal practices (the Alexander technique, Feldenkrais etc.). Shusterman divides the new discipline in three: a) an *analytical* somaesthetics which is descriptive and thematicizing (and where Merleau-Ponty and Foucault may be regarded as prominent exponents); b) a *pragmatic* somaesthetics which is normative and prescriptive, that is, which proposes and discusses methods for somatic improvement. This applies to the aforementioned corporeal therapies, but also various types of yoga, diets, martial arts, erotic techniques; c) a *practical* somaesthetics which involves "practicing methods of somatic care through intelligently disciplined body work aimed at somatic self-improvement". The discipline as a whole shall be a "comprehensive philosophical discipline concerned with self-knowledge and self-care". Where such a discipline might belong in a university system is even discussed.

"Somaesthetics" has practically become a brand name for Shusterman, who travels around the world today and lectures on this as a discipline and also provides courses in corporeal therapy and obviously enjoys the fact that philosophy can again talk about eroticism and sexuality. As an aesthetic thinker he is undoubtedly an important one within pragmatism. Beside Dewey, both Wittgenstein and Foucault count as his sources of inspiration. He wishes philosophy to be work on oneself. More than arguing for a philosophical position, it is a matter of refining the corporeal (sensibility), exposing oneself to new experiences, testing oneself, exceeding and changing oneself. One might ask, however, whether somaesthetics involves something more or other than the hardest of all arts, the art of life.

III

Aisthetics instead of aesthetics?

Aesthetics as a theory of ways of sensing and practices for the sensibilization of the senses, aisthetics, of course has its history. Nietzsche talked of an "aesthetic way of relating", an "aesthetic state", orientated towards the body. Provocatively, now and then after the break with Wagner, he reduced aesthetics to aesthetic physiology, or as Heidegger formulates it critically in his reading of Nietzsche, "He brought art down to the level of the function of stomach juices"

(Heidegger 1961, p. 110). Theodor Lipp's claim at the beginning of the previous century that aesthetics is a psychological discipline belongs to this line of thought or undercurrent which of course includes Fechner [17], Vischer, Helmholtz and other less known people such as Grant Allen, who called his work *Physiological Aesthetics* (1877), based on Darwin's and Spencer's evolution theory etc. ; in other words, the whole "Ästhetik vom unten" tradition, which has a varying degree of scientific pretensions. Previously Brillat-Savarin studied the physiology of taste (1826) and Baudelaire wrote about laughter in this perspective. His "Of the nature of laughter" (1855) originally had the title "The physiology of laughter" (*Physiologie du rire).* Max Dessoir's idea of an "aesthetic science" for "the aesthetic life", and Helmuth Plessner's *Ästhesiologie* (1923) also belong to this *aesthesis* line (cf. *Ästhetische Grundbegriffe* vol 1, p 391). Dessoir was the founder of *Zeitschrift für Ästhetik und Allgemeine Kunstwissenschaft* (1906) and had great influence with international congresses for aesthetics. He distinguished this aesthetic science from the science of art, because he did not see any necessary connection or identity between the beautiful, aesthetics and art. "...the circle of the aesthetic is wider than the field of art" (Dessoir 1905, p. 435). At the same time Dessoir emphasized that aesthetic life included the aesthetic dimension of daily life, which expressed itself in rhythmic structures in an aesthetic experience dependent upon the body.

In 1937, in his opening speech at the second Congrès International d'esthétique et de science de l'Art in Paris, Paul Valéry introduced the term "esthésique", to accentuate the foundation of *aisthesis* and aesthetics with Baumgarten. *Esthésique* was set in contrast to the French metaphysical, in his opinion, fossilized "science du beau". Instead Valéry wanted to have an "étude de la sensation", a study of sensitization which was particularly interested in "the sensory excitations and reactions *that do not have a uniform and well-defined physiological role*" (Valéry 1975, p. 1311). "Aesthesics" was to have the task of studying the defunctionalized sensations, both the pathic and the cognitive aspects, and how these were linked to sensibility, thought and action.

---

[17] Gustav Theodor Fechner, who launched "Aesthetik von Unten" against the metaphysical "Aesthetik von Oben", is especially interesting. He imagined a broad concept of the aesthetic and referred to transcendental aesthetics in Kant's first critique (cf. Welsch above). This aesthetics was to include "all factors related to sensory observation with the scarcely distinguishable relation to physiological and physical factors" (Fechner 1925, p. 33).

The pleasure and desire that accompanied these sensations, and that was not the expression of lack or need, blended sensuality, fertility and energy in a complex and mysterious way (ibid. p.1296). Valéry envisaged a theory of this, à la Aristotle, not a subject or a science (cf. *Ästhetische Grundbegriffe vol 1*, p. 393).

While Valéry conserves the tension in the concept of aesthetics, in Welsch and Böhme the theories lean towards an all-embracing explanation and philosophical fundationalism and go too far in the direction of accepting aestheticisation. In Shusterman we may feel inclined to accept that somaesthetics must have both a professional foundation and be an activity. However, both *aisthetics* and *somaesthetics* should be a *reminder*, neither a new theory (in a strong sense) nor a new, extensive subject area. It is not acceptable to regard Baumgarten and the earlier aesthetics as precursors of pure aisthetics. As regards Baumgarten, if we take his meditations on poetry (1735) and *Aesthetica* (1750) as the foundation of aesthetics[18], we see that 'aesthetics' constitutes a new configuration that is formed between the elements of 'the sensory', 'the beautiful', and 'art'. Until then, these elements had had independent histories.[19] The configuration is formed against the background of a new, modern episteme. In Baumgarten we find an *aisthetic* definition of aesthetics; in that of course those who would renew Baumgarten's project in different ways are correct. But that is not the whole story. Reflection too, the reflective that becomes so clearly expressed in early romanticism, was prepared in the aesthetic, as we can see it manifested in Baumgarten.

In a couple of interesting articles, Christoph Menke (Menke 2000 and 2002) has shown that the experience of the beautiful in Baumgarten is a medium for reflection on the usual sensory acquisition and process. Baumgarten's new definition of the sensory consists of seeing it as a specific activity. This is shown for example by Baumgarten's pointing out that we can *practise* sensory cognition. For practice is something I can only do myself. That is what training is all about: doing it oneself. Even the concept of activity (Tätigkeit) is thus changed with Baumgarten (in relation to rationalism). Menke writes:

---

[18] Baumgarten is rather the one who gives aesthetics its name. The origin is more complex.

[19] For a good description of the aesthetic prior to Baumgarten, see Trond Berg Eriksen 1993. We find a thorough examination of *aisthesis* prior to Plato in Thomas Schirren 1998.

> For in the same way as I can only practise what I can do myself, then I *must* practise only that which I cannot freely master. That is what makes practice necessary: that wanting to do something is not sufficient to be able to do it. Practice is necessary where we are unable to control events and processes through sheer will alone. In this way the exercises stand in contrast to the rules of the method, by which understanding is led. The field of sense concerns actions, which are exclusively based on us, in the subject... However, my sensibilty, also when it is understood as my activity, never belongs "wholly to me". The field of exercises eschews methodical control. Early aesthetics had the concept of 'force' for this. (Menke 2002, p.163f.).

Activity is understood as active forces. In the aesthetic form of sensibility which functions and gives works, a reconnection to the prerequisites for the effects of actions and products takes place, the activity and effects of the forces; after Baumgarten this is made explicit by Mendelssohn and Sulzer and developed by Kant. The forces themselves appear in this reflection; they act and result in works. The reflective movement is not self-recognition, but self-awareness, the feeling of aesthetic pleasure. *Pleasure then, as a reflective definition of the aesthetic.* Thus, the experience of beauty is no longer gradually separated from normal sensory experience, but different from it. What happens further on is that this aesthetic reflection becomes the central definition of works of art (Schlegel, Hegel).

Aestheticisation?

A return to a pure *aisthetics* is therefore problematical, to put it mildly. A pure aisthetic view of aesthetics: that aesthetic processes are merely a variant of forms of sensation, perception and representation, which take place regardless – does not do aesthetic experience or artistic experience justice. Instead of the autonomy of art we get an autonomy of sensibility. Nor then has the extension of the concept of aesthetics that we find for example in Welsch, Böhme and Shusterman gone unopposed either. In particular the extension of the aesthetic in the direction of 'aestheticisation' has caused aestheticians to react negatively or take entrenched positions. After all, "aestheticisation" means making something non-aesthetic aesthetic, or regarding this as aesthetic. "Aestheticisation of world-life" had long been utilized in German. When Welsch launched his theses on aestheticisation processes, at the great "Die Aktualität des Ästhetischen" congress in Hannover in September 1992, Karl Heinz Bohrer opened his speech with the following salvo: "Something terrible straddles the country: Acceptance of the aesthetic". Bohrer's lecture, "Die Grenzen des Ästhetischen" stood in sharp contrast to Welsch's introductory lecture, "Das Ästhetische – eine Schlüsselkategorie unserer Zeit?", where the answer to the question of course was yes.[20] Bohrer, who had always previously defended the aesthetically modern against the politically modern in Habermas' sense, held that "aesthetisization of the life world" involved a levelling of the aesthetic in a narrower sense, of the specific value of the work of art. If the aesthetic is to continue to be an antidote to (the banal) common sense of daily life, the boundaries must again be set. While Bohrer previously found the specifically aesthetic in the self-referential, primary emphasis was placed on the aesthetic experience's "absolute presence", and categories such as 'immediacy', 'appearance', 'epiphany', and 'intensity' are the central ones.[21] In Bohrer such concepts are no longer Utopian.

It is not hard to concede that Bohrer is right in much of what he propounds. A successful universal aestheticisation would be a terrible thing. Art cannot emerge into everyday life to atone for "the plastic force of life" (Nietzsche). Where the boundary between art and non-art is erased by an aestheticizsation of reality, the result is an-aestheticisation, the sedation of the senses and of percetion. One of the tasks of aesthetics is to guard (or perhaps better: monitor) this boundary – the boundary for which the Romans had a special spirit – Terminus; boundary (Lat. *limes*), or better: threshold (Lat. *limen*). The artist himself stands like a Janus on this threshold. On the other hand, nothing would be gained by returning to a traditional, narrow concept of aesthetics. Extension of the concept of aesthetics has come to stay and given us both a broader and deeper insight. The remedy for aestheticisation is aesthetics.

However, on his part Bohrer has a tendency to fix concepts regarding the most overwhelming of aesthetic experiences. This tendency to fix or circle around the ultimate concepts of aesthetics is even clearer in Hans Ulrich Gumbrecht, who in his criticism of hermeneutics attempts to reconstruct the aesthetic experience as an experience of presence; presence's character of anti-mimesis and event (Gumbrecht 2004). There is something "wishful" and gross about Gumbrecht's desire for presence (Gumbrecht 2003, p. 215)

---

[20] The lectures have been collected in W. Welsch (ed), *Die Aktualität des Ästhetischen*, Munich 1993.

[21] Bohrer wrote about the immediate and the aesthetic appearance's moment as early as in 1981. See Bohrer 1981.

which is reflected in the way he calls forth the words – "the intensity of the moment", "epiphany", "presence". The physical dimension connected to this experience is accentuated ad absurdum when Gumbrecht exemplifies his presence-aesthetics through American Football (something that Bohrer would have disdainfully declined). In general Gumbrecht accepts aestheticisation as necessary, not least aestheticisation of the body. In full seriousness he claims that aestheticisation of sport could solve the problem of doping (Gumbrecht 2006).

As a contrast one may merely refer to Barthes or Adorno, where such concepts are not thematicized and isolated, but are brought into play through descriptions and – and as in Adorno – are included as elements in aesthetic configurations that are continually reconfigured (cf. Adorno 1997). As far as the somatic aspect of aesthetic experience is concerned, Adorno is not averse to comparing its culmination with an orgasm. But Adorno was far from reducing aesthetic exprerience to a materialism of the body.

It goes without saying that a total aesthetics or pan-aesthetics must fall apart, both logically and experientally. Perhaps we may wish for "a Sunday in breadth", as Ernst Bloch said, but not a permanent feast, a permanent state of emergency. Borderline experiences remain borderline experiences.

References

Adorno, Th.W. 1997, *Aesthetic Theory*. The Athlone Press, London.

Barthes, R. 1977, *Roland Barthes by Roland Barthes*, Hill and Wang, New York

Barck, K. et al. eds. 2000, ff, *Ästhetische Grundbegriffe* vol 1. Meltzer Verlag, Stuttgart.

Berg Eriksen, T. 1993, "Aisthesis fra Platon til Baudrillard", in: *EST*, Oslo.

Böhme, G. 1995, *Atmosphäre. Essays zur neuen Ästhetik*, Suhrkamp, Frankfurt a. M.

Böhme, G. 2001, *Aisthetik. Vorlesungen über Ästhetik als allgemeine Wahrnehmungslehre*, W. Fink Verlag, Munich.

Bohrer, K.H. 1981, *Plötzlichkeit. Zum Augenblick des ästhetischen Scheins*, Suhrkamp Verlag, Frankfurt a. M.

Danto, A. 1986, *The Philosophical Disenfranchisement of Art*, Columbia University Press.

Danto, A. 2005, "The Future of Aesthetics", ForArt Lecture, Oslo.

Dessoir, M. 1923, *Ästhetik und allgemeine Kunstwissenschaft* (1906), Stuttgart.

Elkins, J.(ed) 2006, *Art History versus Aesthetics*, Routledge, London.

Fechner, G.T. 1925, *Vorschule der Ästhetik* (1876), Vol.1, Leipzig.

Foster, H. 1983, "Postmodernism: A Preface", in: Foster, H. (ed), *The Anti-Aesthetic. Essays on Posmodern Culture*, Bay Press, Washington.

Gumbrecht, H.U. 2003, "Epiphanien", in: J. Küpper and Chr. Menke (eds), *Dimensionen ästhetischer Erfahrung*, Suhrkamp Verlag.

Gumbrecht, H.U. 2004, *Production of Presence. What meaning cannot convey*. Stanford University Press.

Gumbrecht, H.U. 2006, "Schöner, kühner, leichter", Frankfurter Allgeimeine Zeitung, 26/8/06.

Inquiry Vol.48, No. 2, April 2005. pp. 189–200, "Symposium: Arthur Danto, *The Abuse of Beauty*.

M. Kelly ed. 1998, *Encyclopedia of Aesthetics*, four vols., Oxford University Press.

Menke, Chr. 2000, "Modernity, subjectivity and aesthetic reflection", in: Peter Osborne ed., *From an aesthetic point of view*, Serpent's Tail.

Menke, Chr. 2002, "Die Reflexion im Ästhetischen", in: *Zeitschrift für Ästhetik und Allgemeine Kunstwissenschaft* 46/2.

New Left Review 218/1996, 225/1997.

L'Orange, H.P. 1973, "Romersk idyll", in: *Sentrum og periferi*. Dreyers forlag.

Schaeffer, J.-M. 2000, *Adieu à l'esthétique*, PUF, Paris.

Schaeffer, J.-M. 2000, *Art of the Modern age. Philosophy of Art from Kant to Heidegger*, Princeton University Press.

Shusterman, R. 1999, "Somaesthetics: A Disciplinary Proposal", *The Journal of Aesthetics and Art Criticism* 57:3.

Welsch, W. 1996, *Grenzgänge der Ästhetik*, Reclam, Stuttgart.

Welsch, W. (ed) 1993, *Die Aktualität des Ästhetischen*, München.

Liv Hausken

The Aesthetics of X-ray Imaging

X-ray technology was the primary medical imaging technology of the twentieth century. Nevertheless, remarkably little research has been done on this type of image as an aesthetic object. This chapter aims to get closer to an understanding of the aesthetics of x-ray imaging in everyday life. Aesthetics, then, is not viewed as a philosophy of art, but as a theory of culturally embedded sensation and perception. The object chosen for the investigation is the instrumental x-ray image in general, and the chest x-ray in particular. These images will be seen from the perspective of the non-professional. The method could be described as a comparative reflection on the distinction between photography and x-ray imaging. The main reason for this comparison is that in spite of their similarities, I believe that the two types of images have different technical and socio-cultural conditions for their appearance as aesthetic objects. In this chapter I will suggest two major differences. The first relates to the professionalisation of radiology and the second to what is usually thought of in terms of visibility versus invisibility. Together, these two issues form a complex that I believe is important to investigate if we are to understand the conditions for the aesthetics of x-ray imaging today. These conditions are not only different from those pertaining to photography, but also from those of the early days of x-ray imaging.[1]

The discovery of x-rays by Wilhelm Conrad Röntgen in 1895 had a momentous impact, not only within the scientific community, but also on culture at large. Music hall songs were written about it. Stories, poems and caricatures were published in the popular press just after the sensational reports of this new discovery. A mixture of excitement and fear was a major factor in the attraction to the

---

[1] An early version of this text was presented as a paper on the Nordic conference of art history, NORDIK, in Bergen, Norway, September 22.-24. 2006. I am grateful to the members of the research project Photography in Culture for their comments on a draft of this chapter.

x-ray technology and the images that were produced, published and raved about.

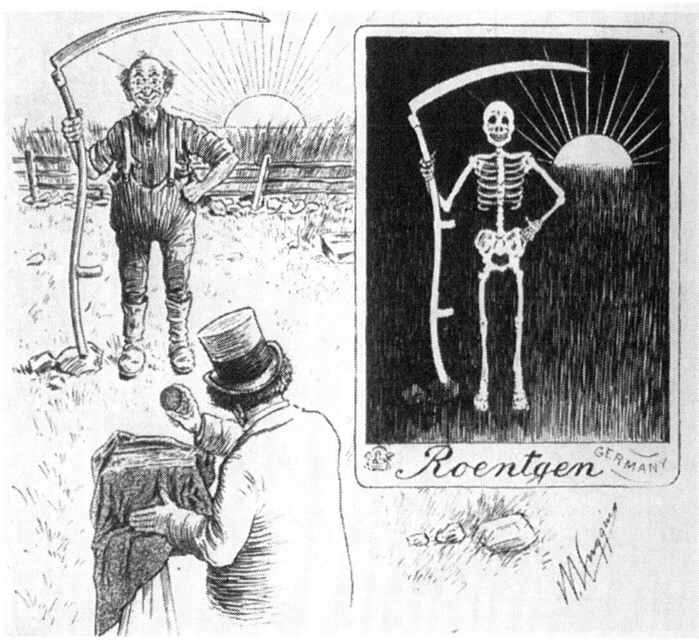

Figure 1. The new roentgen photography. "Look pleasant, please".

This cartoon was published in the 1896 magazine *Life* two months after Röntgen's discovery of x-rays.[2] It presents a scene where a farmer with his scythe is posing in his everyday work clothes for the photographer early in the morning. In front of this scene we are shown what is supposed to be the result of the picture making process, an image of the very much alive ordinary man and his agricultural tool transformed into the Grim Reaper. The caption is twofold: The first is a label on the new image technology itself, at the time commonly known as "the new photography", here specifically connected to Röntgen's discovery of the x-rays. The second is the photographer's line, "Look pleasant, please". This cartoon is a typical manifestation of the public's interest, revealing a mixture of fascination and fear. It also illustrates the spontaneous association of photography and x-ray imaging by the combination of a photographer and an x-ray image, by the caption's designation of x-ray imaging as different from

---

[2] *Life*, February 27, 1896, p.155. Cf. also *Electrical Engineer*, no. 23, p.464, 1897.

photography, and also by the x-ray-photographer's unnecessary invitation to smile, since the grin of the skeleton is unavoidable.

The cartoon has been reprinted in a large number of publications on x-rays and x-ray imaging,[3] very often without any comment or with a slightly ambiguous note, as for instance in Richard F. Mould's richly illustrated historical overview of x-rays and radioactivity in medicine, where the author remarks: "Unfortunately the artist got it wrong: X-rays are not reflected back from the subject towards the X-ray tube and photographic plate!"[4] The comparison of the visible light of photography and the invisible light involved in the production of the x-ray image is quite correct: X-radiation is not reflected, but absorbed in different degrees by different materials.[5] The rays that are not totally absorbed form a negative image as they transmit the object and hit the photosensitive plate. A radiograph is therefore a shadowgraph. The remark thus points to a rather sophisticated part of the joke that may not even have been intentional, since the nature of the new rays was not known at the time.[6] As an alternative to seeing Mould's remark as a serious comment on what he believed to be a serious and mistaken conception of the new imaging technology, it may also be understood as an inside joke among physicists that deliberately ignores what the 1896 cartoon is more obviously about: the widespread impression that x-ray imaging technology allowed people to steal a glance at their future fate as skeletons, a theme commented on by almost anyone writing about the popular imagination of x-rays.[7]

The composite image of the pre-photographic scene, the photographer and the final picture may also be seen as pointing towards the changing view of reality at the time of the introduction of x-rays: until then photography was seen as an instrument for showing the

---

[3] Cf. for instance Knight 1986, p.16; Eisenberg 1992, p.587; Glasser 1993, p.42; Mould 1993, p.9; McClafferty 2001, p.23.

[4] Mould 1993, p.9.

[5] X-rays are not reflected in the way visible light is reflected, and that is what matters here. Cf. Saxby 2002, p.235 on how x-rays nevertheless can be reflected from metals at grazing incidents.

[6] The rather odd position of the sun in front of the camera may however indicate that it was known that the rays were not reflective, but that they would in this case by analogy pass from the sun through the farmer's body and make a shadow on the photographic plate of the photographer.

[7] Cf. for instance van Dijck 2005, p.93-97; McClafferty 2001, p.20-31; Cartwright 1995, p.114; Knight 1986; Grove 1997.

nature of physical reality, but now the x-ray demonstrated the possibility of revealing a nature formerly unseen, and thereby displaced the idea of what could be seen as real. This shift made it possible to contemplate not only the reality of hidden parts of the living body, but also the reality of spirits and ghosts. In the words of José van Dijck, "X rays were believed to be a sort of super-photography that could prove the existence of immaterial substances, the materiality of things heretofore unseen."[8] In historical retrospect, this is sometimes denounced as quackery, as for instance in an otherwise well-informed article by the physicist Graham Farmelo at the hundredth anniversary of the discovery of x-rays, where attempts at "photographing the soul" are juxtaposed with advertisements for "x-ray proof underclothing" and reports on the possibility of transforming "a 13-cent piece of metal into gold worth $ 153."[9] However, the idea of photographing the soul using the new imaging technology may be seen as an appropriate extension of the belief that photographing the soul was already possible using well-known, sixty year old photographic techniques.[10] As pointed out by Lisa Carthwright, "The technique that Roentgen introduced with his X-ray experiments was the subject of public hysteria not because it was shockingly new but because it ushered into the realm of science a disturbing technique of bodily representation long circulating in areas less invested than physics with epistemological authority – namely, popular metaphysics and public entertainment."[11] In "Röntgen's Ghosts: Photography, X-Rays, and the Victorian Imagination", Allen Grove examines the way in which Röntgen's discovery of x-rays confirmed many pre-existing ideas about the existence of ghosts and the way in which the photographic plate could detect realities invisible to the human eye. The article situates Röntgen's discovery within a history of ghost fiction, ghost hunting, and ghost-like photographs. According to Grove, "Science could not kill the ghost easily. In fact, science was to a degree the ally of ghosts."[12] Many of the members of the Society of Psychical Research were both scientists and spiritualists, including its leader, William Crookes, the very same Crookes as the one who

---

8 van Dijck 2005, p.17.
9 Farmelo 1995, p.89.
10 Cf. for instance Grove 1997, p.154. Cf. Cheroux et.al. 2005.
11 Cartwright 1995,113.
12 Grove 1997, p.141.

gave his name to the x-ray tube involved in Röntgen's discovery.[13] One of the primary goals of the Society was to discover real ghosts in contrast to frauds. According to Nancy Knight's discussion of x-rays and medical futurism, "The discovery of x-rays coincided with a rise in public interest in psychic and supernatural phenomena, and soon the new technology and the old preoccupation were linked".[14] These rather blurred boundaries between science and spiritualism around the turn of the last century may explain the overwhelming reaction to a scientific discovery.

It has been argued that Röntgen's publication of his findings at the end of December 1895 triggered the most immediate and widespread reaction to any scientific discovery before the explosion of the first atomic bomb in 1945.[15] Both these two moments in history can be related to two of the very few strongly symbolic x-ray images in history: the first being the x-ray image of Bertha Röntgen's hand published in newspapers worldwide with her husband's first report on the discovery of the unknown rays, and the second being the x-ray impressions of Hiroshima and Nagasaki A-bomb victims. As underlined by Bettyann Holtzmann Kevles, "Only after 1945 – fifty years after the publication of the image of Frau Roentgen's skeletal hand – did an X-ray image take center stage again, but this time it was the X-rayed silhouettes of the dead blasted into slabs of concrete in the ruins of Hiroshima".[16] But even if there are not many x-ray images that can compete in symbolic strength with these two images, it is striking how the public reaction to the discovery of x-rays is connected to an intense fascination with the x-ray *pictures*.[17] This allegedly frustrated Röntgen himself, because he was far more interested in discovering the true nature and properties of the rays.[18] The public's interest in the nature of the rays may have been rather low, but both scientists and the public seem to agree that Röntgen had discovered a new way of looking. According to van Dijck, both doctors and the general public had to adjust their gaze "to a changing

[13] cf for instance Grove 1997, p.142; Kevles 1997, p.119.
[14] Knight 1986, p.18.
[15] Badash 1979, p.9. Cf. also Henderson 1988, p.324.
[16] Kevles 1997, p.141. It may be worth mentioning that it took almost a decade for people to associate the horrors of bomb-wrought diseases with the benevolence of x-ray images. cf. for instance Kevles 1997, p.262.
[17] Cf. Reiser 1978, pp.58-68. Cf. also Lerner 1992.
[18] cf. Farmelo 1995, p.89.

scopic regime".[19] While the idea that x-rays represent a new way of looking has been included in studies of x-rays in the popular imagination and in more general studies of modern visuality, the x-ray image as such has only to a limited extent been the focus of interest.

To my knowledge, there does not exist any comprehensive work on the aesthetics of x-ray imaging. There are comments on the issue to be found in critical studies of medical history: Lisa Cartwright's study of cinematic technologies and medical experiments (1995); Bettyann Holtzmann Kevles' history of x-ray imaging and subsequent developments in medicine, art and popular imagination (1997); and more recently José van Dijck's cultural analysis of medical imaging (2005). There are also valuable comments on x-ray imaging in the scientific and popular imagination as well as in popular fiction in the previously mentioned articles by Nancy Knight (1986) and Allen Grove (1997). Also worth mentioning is the contribution of Linda Dalrymple Henderson (1988, 1989, 2002) to the understanding of x-ray aesthetics in modern visual art. However, there seems to be a tendency to focus on the ideas and fantasies about x-rays and x-ray imaging in art and culture, rather than on the image itself and on how the ideas and fantasies contribute to the constitution of this particular image. Studies of Thomas Mann's novel *The Magic Mountain* (1924) have for some reason been the exception to this rule.[20] In the visual arts, Robert Rauschenberg's *Booster* (1967) should also be mentioned as a work of art where commentators have paid attention to the fact that real x-ray images were involved in the production,[21] in contrast to, for instance, the avant-garde art studied by Henderson. Generally speaking, however, these undertakings have not focused on what characterises the x-ray image as an aesthetic object. This will be done here.

Like the explosion of the first atomic bomb in 1945, the discovery of x-rays produced a sense that the world had changed irrevocably. Yet, as Henderson has pointed out, over the decades following World War I, the novelty of x-ray images and the turn-of-the-century awareness of the scientific and philosophical ramifications of x-rays steadily waned. "Thus", she proclaims, "when Robert Rauschenberg used a full-body x-ray of himself in his 1967 print

---

19 van Dijck 2005, p.85.

20 Cf. van Dijck 2005, p.85-99 and Cartwright 1995 s.123-125. See also Kevles 1997, p.121; Henderson 1988, p.325; Grove 1997, p.162 and 165.

21 Kevles, p.271-273, 313. Cf also Henderson 1988, p.336.

Booster, viewers recognized the image immediately as a variation on their own routine medical experiences or those of others. Gone were the sense of awe and wonder, the sudden awareness of the relativity of perception, and the fascination with the dematerialization of matter that had characterized the pre-World War I response to x rays."[22] Nevertheless, I will argue that although the initial enormous response to x-rays must clearly be seen as part of the historical past, and although the idea of a dematerialisation of matter has taken several new twists after both the First and Second World Wars and after the introduction of the computer into everyday life, there is still something intriguing about this image that cannot be reduced or confined to the ideas of the avant-garde and what has been characterised as the search for the invisible in early modern art.[23] On the contrary, I believe that the fact that viewers of Rauchenberg's *Booster* most likely recognised the image immediately as a variation on their own routine medical experiences is an important dimension of the aesthetics of x-ray imaging today. The aesthetic qualities of x-ray imaging have changed over time. When x-ray technology was new, the image of a skeletal hand was spontaneously identified with death; after thirty years and in an age of social responsibility and the growing problem of tuberculosis, the image of clean lungs was the reassuring image of good health; after more than one hundred years, and in an age of growing anxiety and personal responsibility, what do these x-ray images look like?

The first step towards conceptualising the aesthetics of x-ray imaging will be to get closer to an understanding of what kind of image we are talking about. This will be done through a comparison with photography. This comparison is made for several reasons. As the cartoon above suggests, x-ray imaging was immediately associated with photography, and this was not simply a historical coincidence. The two images are strikingly similar in more than one way. Keeping the two apart may therefore be seen as an opportunity to get a better grip of them both. Furthermore, and this is a hypothesis, I believe that the two types of images have different technical and socio-cultural conditions for their appearance as aesthetic objects. To compare x-ray imaging with photography may therefore help us to

[22] Henderson 1988, p.336.
[23] Cf. Henderson 2002 and Clarke and Henderson 2002, p.96-97.

approach an understanding of the x-ray image as an object of sensation and perception.

Photographic and x-ray imaging may be considered *similar techniques of imaging*: they both visually display the distribution of something physically existing at the moment of exposure. This similarity is even more apparent if we compare the x-ray image to photographs taken without a camera (sometimes termed photograms). Both images are made by placing an object directly onto the surface of a photosensitive material and then exposing it to light. In both cases, the result is a silhouetted image varying in darkness based on the transparency of the objects used, with areas of the photo-sensitive material that have *not* received any light appearing light and those that *have* received light appearing dark. Hence, and in both cases, the image obtained is a negative. The light involved is different in the two cases: both x-rays and visible light are electromagnetic radiation, but with different frequencies.[24] Furthermore, camera-based photography involves *reflected* light rather than light *transmitting* the object. These technical differences make an aesthetic difference. It is often thought of as a difference between the visible and the invisible, a distinction that needs to be problematised and qualified before it can contribute to an understanding of contemporary x-ray aesthetics. There is, however, a different kind of difference between photography and x-ray imaging that must be developed before we come back to this issue of visibility, the question of professionalisation.

During the first fifteen years after Röntgen's discovery of x-rays in 1895, there was an intimate relationship between radiologists and photographers.[25] Photographers without any medical training opened x-ray studios and called their sessions x-ray sittings. They considered the x-ray imaging process a natural extension of their medium, and how-to manuals and photography journal articles proliferated during 1896 and thereafter, along with new suppliers specialising in x-ray equipment.[26] It was not until the 1910s that radiology emerged as a medical profession, thus forcing the photographers out of business.[27] Before the First World War, anyone had been allowed to do radiological work. According to Arne Hessenbruch's study of calibration and work in the x-ray economy during the first three decades

[24] cf. for instance Mackay 1984, p.83.
[25] Cf. for instance Hessenbruch 2000 p.397 and p.406.
[26] cf for instance Henderson, 1988, p.325 and 334.
[27] cf van Dijck 2005 p.92.

after the discovery of the rays, the discipline was professionalised shortly after the war in the sense that independent lay radiological work "was outlawed and, in Britain for example, a postgraduate radiology course was initiated."[28] Some may object that lay radiology was neither illegal nor illegitimate after the war, particularly if we think of the shoe-fitting fluoroscope, which reached its peak of popularity in the early 1950s, used by ordinary shoe store employees without any training or protection. As suggested by Jacalyn Duffin and Charles R.R.Hayter, this may be seen as an example of the triumph of capitalism over common sense.[29] It is, however, important to note that independent lay radiological work was *marginalised* with the professionalisation of radiology, and that medicine seems to have been able to force *competitive* radiological work out of business.[30] This professionalisation and incorporation of radiology into the medical profession that ended the historically intimate relationship between radiologists and photographers may be considered as a first step towards a specialisation of the competent and legitimate gaze towards x-ray images, a specialisation that I will argue informs all the other possible ways of looking at an x-ray image, including the aesthetic gaze.

The professionalisation of radiology is in other words important in terms of the conditions for an aesthetic gaze towards x-ray images. By looking at the conditions for an aesthetic gaze directed towards a particular image, we may contribute to an understanding of the constitution of the aesthetics of the x-ray image. The object chosen for the investigation is an object that we normally do not think of in aesthetic terms, namely what I will call the *instrumental x-ray image*. This choice is made in preference to the x-ray art of Rauchenberg,[31] or more recent examples like *The Three Monolithic Religions* (2005) and the self-portrait (2004) of the Asian-American artist Hady Sy[32] or the project *X = t* (1995) by the Japanese artist Seiju Toda.[33] These

---

[28] cf. Hessenbruch 2000 p.410.

[29] Cf. Duffin and Hayter, 2000, p.281.

[30] As to the professionalization of radiology, see also the comparative work of Halpern (1992).

[31] *Booster* (1967), *Sky Garden* (1969) and the series *Sling Shot* (1984-85). Cf. Kevles, p.271-273, 313.

[32] http://www.ecfa.com/site/artists.php?aid=109 [last checked January 23, 2007] cf also http://www.hadysy.com/ last checked January 23, 2007]

[33] Seiju Toda (1995) *X = t: the art of X-ray photography*, (Introduction by Max Kozloff), N.Y.: Hudson Hills Press.

artworks may be informative as to the aesthetics of x-ray imaging, but they are at the same time embedded in an art discourse. What I am looking for is an aesthetics of x-ray imaging outside the fine arts. The instrumental x-ray image is produced for a particular function, and because of the professionalisation of radiology this is a function performed by a specialist. Any object can serve several functions, including an aesthetic function. This also goes for the instrumental x-ray image. This image may therefore be studied from the perspective of the specialist as to its possible tension between different functions. We can, however, also look at the tension between different functions from a perspective outside both the art world and the corridors of radiological specialists, and focus on the aesthetics of the instrumental x-ray image in everyday life. As a point of departure I will therefore give an example of an x-ray image very much out there in the street: the concept t-shirt, or to be more specific: the x-ray image t-shirt.

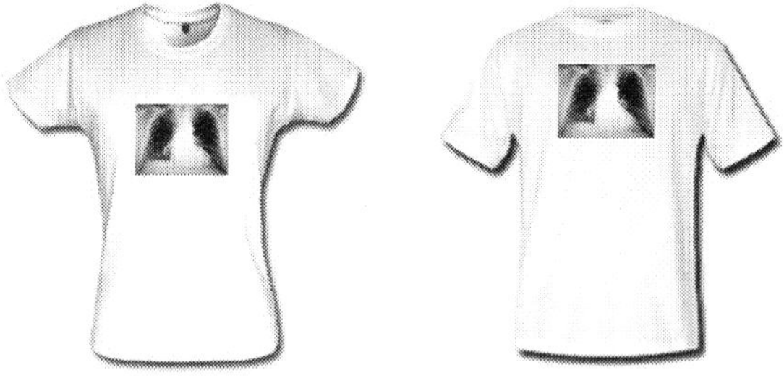

Figure 2. Chest X-ray, ConceptTshirts.co.uk[34].

The motif of this concept t-shirt illustrates what I believe is the most common idea of the x-ray image, that is: the chest x-ray. As an image on a t-shirt for commercial distribution, it is a clear example of an *anonymous* chest x-ray.[35] This anonymous chest x-ray image will be the point of departure in the following discussion of the aesthetics of x-ray imaging.

The anonymous chest x-ray image falls within what I call instrumental x-ray images. This is a rather comprehensive category

---

[34] http://www.spreadshirt.net/shop.php?sid=52345&search[text]=chestx1 [last checked January 23, 2007]

[35] In addition to refer to the general idea of the x-ray image, the anonymous chest x-ray can be found in historical atlases of x-ray images, in medical and general lexica and encyclopaedias.

of x-ray imaging, including not only x-ray imaging for medical diagnostics, but also for medical illustration, medical experiment and medical surgery, as well as for non-medical applications like airport security screening and the screening of art works to establish authenticity or for conservation purposes.

The fact that the instrumental x-ray image is produced to fill a particular function also implies that it is arranged for a particular gaze, which we may call an analytic gaze. To discuss the conditions for an aesthetic of the instrumental x-ray image, we need to study the social conditions for an aesthetic gaze towards this instrumental image, a gaze that contributes to the constitution of the image as an aesthetic object.

In the following, I will tentatively distinguish between an analytic and an aesthetic gaze, the first gaze primarily associated with detection, examination and diagnostics and the latter gaze primarily associated with engagement with the picture as an artefact with sensuous qualities, rather than as a picture being used as an instrument for detection. We are not talking about different pictures, but different ways of looking at the same picture. Obviously, there are also other ways of looking, but hopefully this distinction can be productive.

The term 'analytic' indicates a process of taking the bits and pieces apart to have a closer look at them (cf. dissection). I will here, however, include in the concept of an analytic gaze an attitude towards the instrumental picture that I believe is logically prior to the analysis of what it actually depicts. As asserted by Klaus Amann and Karin Knorr-Cetina in an article on image dissection in natural science inquiry, "Scientists rarely argue in image-attached conversations. *In dissecting the object, they prefer to point.*"[36] This indexicality or deictic language of image detection is an important dimension of what I here will call an analytic gaze.

Both photography and x-ray imaging may seem to *invite* this pointing gesture. Considered as signs, both images are themselves pointing towards something physically existing at the moment of exposure. As signs, they are "genuine indexes", if we may apply the semiotic language of Charles Sander Peirce. Peirce distinguishes between two types of indexes, the one just pointing towards something and the other pointing towards something that has caused its existence.[37]

---

[36] Knorr-Cetina and Amman, 1990, p.263. Italics in the original text.

[37] Peirce, "A Syllabus of Certain Topics of Logic", EP 2:274 (1903).

The former index (the degenerate index) refers to the way that for instance a portrait, regardless of medium, points towards a particular person, or the way that a graphic sign of a man, a woman and a wheelchair may point you in the direction of a public toilet. The latter index is the index of photographs and x-ray images. This is the index very much used and abused as a term in theories of photography.

Photographs and x-ray images may of course also be seen as pointing towards fictional characters or abstract ideas and may thus in various ways be studied as degenerate indexes. The deictic language of image detection may in these cases be part of the analytic attitude towards these images just as it would be part of the analytic attitude towards any image. The point here is that the genuine index of photography and x-ray images seems to invite a pointing gesture on the part of the viewer towards the image as an *effect* of the referent of the genuine index, in Peirce's terms the object of the indexical sign. Whereas an analytic attitude towards images generally invites the analyst to point at different elements in the image, the analytic attitude towards photography and x-ray images also invites the analyst to recognise the shapes pointed at as a visual display of the distribution of something physically existing in front of the photographic camera or inside the x-rayed body at the moment of exposure.

What I have here tentatively described as an *analytic* gaze towards photographs and x-ray images has a striking similarity to what we may call the *everyday* gaze towards the family photo and most other non-art photographs. Whereas the radiologist or physicist points at the picture and says, "this is a broken rib" or "hey, we have found the lost scissors", most of us will point at the family photograph and say: "this is uncle Arthur on his fiftieth birthday." This everyday gaze towards the family photos is not analytic; it is not directed towards examination or critical analysis. But what it has in common with this analytical gaze is the act of pointing.

The *aesthetic* gaze towards pictures is not primarily concerned with this pointing gesture. Neither is it particularly concerned with specific references to empirical facts indicated by the image. A portrait, for instance, may be valued even when its subject cannot be identified. The identification of the subject of the portrait is not of primary interest to the aesthetic gaze. This is rather a way of looking at the picture as a picture; it is, (if I may use a word that is probably better known among literary scholars than in research on images), a gaze directed towards the pictorialness of the picture.

This aesthetic gaze can be directed towards any picture, including a family photo, in the same way as the detecting or analytic attitude can be directed towards any picture, including the photo of uncle Arthur, in which case we may reveal that he is not actually the man in the photo at all, or that it was taken not on his birthday but on Christmas Eve. Neither the genuine nor the degenerate index of, for instance, a photographic portrait is a proof of whom the portrait depicts or what was actually in front of the camera.[38] As Peirce has made clear, the deictic language of the indexical sign does not do anything but point: "The index asserts nothing; it only says 'There!' It takes hold of our eyes, as it were, and forcibly directs them to a particular object, and there it stops."[39] As an index, this is all it says. To know for sure *what* it is pointing at, we need knowledge of the object. As for any object, it is constituted by knowledge. The point here is to analytically distinguish between two different gazes and to try to conceptualise how the tension between these two gazes influences the aesthetics of x-ray imaging.

Some may object (to this distinction between two gazes) that science and aesthetics have been developed side by side and have influenced each other's gazes. With a reference to the Canadian media scholar Kim Sawchuk, José van Dijck underlines that art and medicine "have worked in tandem in the production of knowledge of our bio-being, not only to produce specific representations, but to develop a particular way of knowing through techniques of visualization".[40] However, the distinction between art and medicine has not disappeared; the two fields have not conflated, and neither have their two gazes: they serve different functions. José van Dijck herself presents some examples of how the same image may serve several functions. I quote: "A colorful, retouched PET scan on the cover of a professional medical journal serves both an educational and an aesthetic function; an ultrasound scan in the logo of a news item on health care exemplifies a purely symbolic use. The use of medical

[38] The photographic portrait can for instance depict a queen, a fictional character, or a real uncle and the photograph can be a trace, that is a technical effect (cf. genuine index) of a model, an actor or an uncle-look-alike. The photograph does not prove the existence of any of this.

[39] Peirce, "On the Algebra of Logic: A Contribution to the Philosophy of Notation", W 5:162-3 (1885).

[40] Sawchuk, quoted by van Dijck 2005 p.11.

images wavers between data sharing and entertainment."[41] What I am interested in is the possible *tension* between the different gazes.

It may be correct that visual depiction of anatomical data, even today, is defined as much by medical technologies as by artistic traditions and styles, as José van Dijck[42] and others have argued. Nevertheless, it seems to me that we not only need to create analytically useful distinctions between fields or functions that seem to merge, but also to have a closer look at how the scientific gaze and medical discourse influence aesthetics. More or less in passing, van Dijck makes a comment that I find very suggestive in this respect. I quote: "Frequent use of X-ray shadows in advertisements or of endoscopic images in motion pictures has not familiarized the audience with their medical interpretation, but has added a variety of connotations to their pictorial styles".[43] In the following I will try to explain why I find this suggestive.

During the first years after the discovery of x-rays, the images produced were assumed to be understandable to everyone. It may appear paradoxical that the idea of the x-ray image as a clear gaze into the living body loses its strength in inverse proportion to the quality of the picture. But the strange thing is that the poor quality of the images did not seem to hinder the idea that normal people on a general level were able to see what the images displayed.[44] It seems reasonable to assume that the view of x-ray imaging as a natural extension of photography added the well-known perceptions of photography to the new image, including the idea that, to be able to look at and understand these images, the viewer does not need greater expertise than is basically provided by one's everyday experience with our physical surroundings. For x-ray imaging this is no longer the case. The first term for the x-ray print was *skiagram*, literally meaning a figure formed by the shadow of an object.[45] To a certain extent, it seems possible to trace changing ideas on the general comprehensibility of x-ray images to changing attitudes towards the term *skiagram* and the figure of the shadow. This is a change from the idea that "Shadows do not lie" from the first decade of the century to the idea that a

41 van Dijck 2005, p.13.
42 van Dijck 2005, p.11.
43 van Dijck 2005, p.12.
44 This is not to say that there weren't discussions about the interpretations of x-ray images among specialists also in the early years of radiology.
45 Cf. for instance Lerner 1992, p.386.

term emphasising shadows suggested haziness and lack of clarity. By the 1920s, x-ray images were no longer hazy, on the contrary, they represented the gold standard of diagnosis for many diseases.[46] With the professionalisation of radiology, the idea of a general competence in understanding x-ray images disappeared from the public view. By 1940, according to Kevles, x-ray images were "redefined by radiology professors and medico-legal experts as too complicated for ordinary people to look at and understand."[47]

I believe this professionalisation of the analytic gaze towards medical x-ray images is one of two major differences between photography and x-ray images in terms of the different conditions for them to appear as aesthetic objects. In sharp contrast to the x-ray image, no-one has claimed the exclusive right to make proper interpretations of the photographic image. On the contrary, photography is the most everyday image that exists, and it is generally assumed to be understandable to everyone.

The second major different condition for their appearance as aesthetic objects concerns an issue often thought of as a distinction between the visible and the invisible: It is said that photography gives access to the visible world while the x-ray image makes invisible objects visible. Both of these ideas need modifications.

Photography gives visual access to the visible world, but it may also give visual access to a physical world invisible to the unaided eye. For instance, microphotography, astronomical photography and high-speed photography are all photographic techniques that give visual access to physical phenomena that lie outside of common visual experience. Secondly, even if it is true that photography gives visual access to the visible world, it does not do so in the same way as the human eye gives visual access to the visible world.[48] The rationale underlying the idea of a fundamental link between photography and the visible world is actually the visible light involved in the photographic process, and the fact that the conceptual distinction between visible and invisible light is made according to a human scale as to what is visible or invisible to the human eye.

X-ray imaging, on the other hand, gives visual access, not to something invisible (as is normally suggested), but to something hidden.

---

46 Cf. Lerner 1992, p.386-87.
47 Kevles 1997, p.141.
48 Cf. for instance Allen and Snyder 1975. Cf. also Crary 1988.

As Ann Thomas has pointed out, x-ray imaging is "the visualisation of hidden structures or sub-visible worlds in science".[49] This may be contrasted with the historical views of both x-rays and photography as technologies that can make the invisible spirits visible.[50] It is the rays that are invisible, not the physical objects that they give visual access to.

To a certain extent and quite contrary to the popular idea that photography presents the visible while x-ray imaging transforms the invisible into something visible, we may say that it is photography, and not the x-ray image, that transforms something invisible to the human eye – that is, imperceptible to human vision because it is too small, too distant or too rapidly moving[51] – into something visually accessible. For the sake of the argument, let us nevertheless operate with an adjusted distinction between the visible and the hidden as a distinction of importance for the different conditions for photography and x-ray images to appear as aesthetic objects.

Furthermore, the distinction between the visible and the hidden must be qualified before it can contribute to an understanding of contemporary x-ray aesthetics. This qualification, I will argue, may be done through a discussion of the complex relationship between this duality of the visible and the hidden and the question of professionalisation outlined above.

Accessibility is a keyword for both of the distinctions between photography and x-ray imaging discussed here. Photography has a high degree of accessibility: photographs surround us in our everyday life. We make them, take them, send them and receive them on a regular basis, and they are used in practically any sphere of society filling a whole range of different functions. Furthermore, in the case of photography, we normally have visual access to what is displayed: we may recognise the object displayed as a physical object from our own world. No-one ever claimed the exclusive right to explain what a photographic image displays. On the contrary, it is a widely held view that there is very little we need to learn before we are able to

---

49 Cf. Thomas, 1997, p.112.

50 This distinction between the invisibility of ghosts and the hidden structures made visible by x-ray imaging may also help to clarify what is at stake in the aesthetics of the allegedly invisible in early modern art. I will not follow up this subject here.

51 cf. microphotography, astronomical photography, and high speed photography respectively.

look at a photograph and identify what it displays.[52] The situation for x-ray imaging is quite different.

Since x-ray technology was rather simple and the equipment was easily available, initially many believed that x-ray imaging would become part of everyday culture,[53] and to a certain extent the x-ray image actually did. As part of their own routine medical experiences, many people have access to a limited amount of x-ray images. There is also public access to anonymous x-ray images in textbooks, medical encyclopaedia, etc. But because of the professionalisation of radiology, there is minimal access to the production and interpretation of these images.

To better understand the aesthetics of x-ray imaging we need to have a closer look at this multifaceted inaccessibility. Here it may be interesting to compare not only x-ray images to photography, but also the medical x-ray image to the luggage scan.

The airport security screening of travellers' luggage is intended to efficiently discover something hidden, which for security reasons shouldn't be there. This question of efficiency is also important for medical, diagnostic x-ray imaging. It is faster, cheaper and less painful to take a picture to find a bullet than to open up the body and look around in there. Both the gun in the suitcase and the bullet in the chest are physically accessible without x-ray or other image technologies: these objects are hidden, and not invisible as such. In principle, they could both also have been physically accessible to the public: the suitcase can be opened and the gun removed in public, in the same way that bullets in human bodies were removed in public at the anatomical theatres during the Renaissance. Immediately after the discovery of x-rays, the x-ray images were also made publicly accessible. There were public performances with x-rays during the first half of the 1896. According to Hessenbruch, x-ray shows were fairly common in most large cities of Europe and America in this period.[54] But after the specialisation and institutionalisation of radiological practice in medicine, this public access to medical x-ray images was heavily reduced. So, it is not only easier to get a gun out of a suitcase

---

52 I am not discussing the question of meaning or interpretation here; just the ability to identify what the common photograph is pointing towards in the visible world of physical objects.

53 Cf. for instance Knight 1986, p.14-18; cf. also Kevles 1997, particularly p.122 and 141.

54 Hessenbruch 2000 p.405-406.

than a bullet out of a human body. It is also easier now than earlier in x-ray history to get public, visual access to the x-ray images of objects hidden in carry-on baggage than of objects hidden beneath the skin of human beings.

In addition to the contrast between the public and the specialist in terms of physical accessibility, there is also a question of knowledge, common or public knowledge versus the knowledge of the specialist. If it is true we have learned to believe that x-ray images are too complicated for ordinary people to look at and understand, it seems reasonable to assume that this may have some relevance not only for the medical x-ray images but also for the luggage scan and for other professional and instrumental uses of x-ray technology. Anyone who has been a victim of suspicion at airport security screening can testify that nearly anything can be mistaken for a knife if it is seen on the screen from the most unlikely of angles. The fact that this mistake does not happen all the time says a great deal about the competence of the analyst watching the screen and interpreting the shapes and the colours of the computerised information. However, bearing out the comparison with photography, even if it may be hard to recognise the objects displayed on the security screen as physical objects from our own world, they are nevertheless objects from a world of visually familiar objects. This may be contrasted to the objects displayed in a medical x-ray image. As Neil Walsh Allen and Joel Snyder have remarked: "[...] no surgeon expects to find anything resembling an x-ray when he opens up a body."[55] The public is cut off not only from the surgeon's ability to understand what is inside a human body but also from the radiologist's knowledge of the x-ray image of this body. This absence of analytical competence outside of the radiology profession influences the aesthetics of x-ray imaging.

I will argue that the absence of analytical competence makes it easier for the x-ray image than for the photograph to appear as an aesthetic object. Let me again contrast the medical x-ray image with the luggage scan. Whereas the colour codes of the luggage scan heighten the analyst's ability to comprehend the display, the lack of competence in the public leaves the common viewer with the coloured shapes of trivial objects. This may point in the direction of a popular aesthetic of transparent handbags for 14 years old girls. In the same way that the re-sealable plastic bags of maximum one litre

---

[55] Allen and Snyder 1975, p.159.

capacity allowed through the security check at (European) airports may stimulate curiosity towards the intimately important items of one's fellow passengers, the transparent handbag demonstratively reveals what we all expect to find in a handbag of a young girl, but nevertheless normally consider to be private. The security screening that breaks publicly into the privacy of every handbag may stimulate a similar curiosity towards the private but well-known items, visually displayed in a public and ordinary but at the same time defamiliarising manner.

Our incompetence towards the chest x-ray seems to point in a different direction. I believe that due to the professionalisation of the analytic gaze in medicine, the absence of analytical competence outside of the profession makes it easier for the *anonymous* chest x-ray image to appear as an aesthetic object. X-ray images of one's *own* body or the bodies of people one knows, on the other hand, leave the viewer in a rather awkward position. Confronted with an absence of analytical competence, these images may appear overwhelmingly and frustratingly poor. The chosen gaze is the analytic gaze, but because of one's lack of knowledge, the image appears as a flat and hazy surface. This non-communicating surface will not normally trigger an aesthetic gaze. However, I will argue that the anonymous chest x-ray seems to stimulate an aesthetic gaze and amplify the aesthetic character of the x-ray image.[56] This is, however, not the same aesthetics as the aesthetics of the luggage scan.

One of the reasons for this is the difference in accessibility discussed above: the public access to the objects hidden in the trunk in contrast to the skin and flesh covering the bone structure; the relative access to the images and to what they display. A second reason for the aesthetic difference between the chest x-ray and the luggage scan is the distinction between living objects and man-made objects. Let me again distinguish the anonymous chest x-ray from the private and individual x-ray image.

Like any x-ray image, the chest x-ray is an effect of one particular x-ray exposure. The x-ray image is therefore pointing towards a specific physical body at a particular place at a certain moment in

[56] Exceptions may be cases where the individual or type is clearly present, such as in a hurt body part like a crushed foot or in the early x-ray images of a newborn baby seen retrospectively with the knowledge that the hazardous rays probably killed the baby. Exceptions like these confirm the rule: it is hard to appreciate the aesthetic qualities of the picture if confronted with individual suffering.

time. But no image can be reduced to its genuine indexicality. The *personal* chest x-ray belongs to a personal history of medical health care. It points towards the individual body and the distinctive detail assumed to be located in that body (even if imperceptible to the untrained eye) and which motivated the production of the image in the first place. The *anonymous* chest x-ray, meanwhile, seems to represent an image of the human body in general.

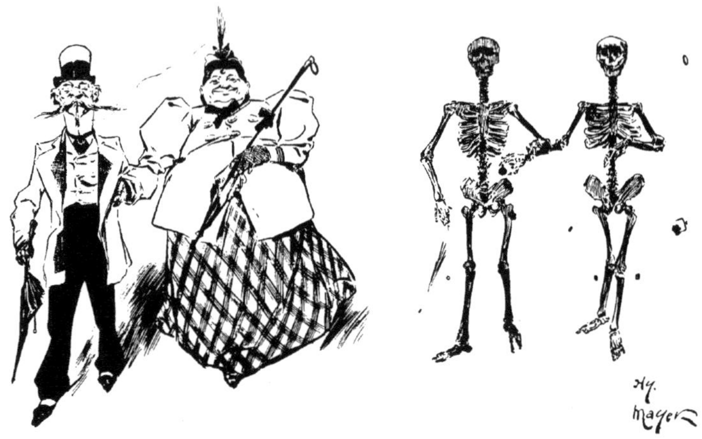

Figure 3. Whether stout or thin, the x-ray makes the whole world kin.

This is an idea just as old as the discovery of x-rays, and may be illustrated by this 1897 cartoon presenting the skinny man and the fat woman and a caption declaring: "whether stout or thin, the x-ray makes the whole world kin".[57] The caption to this cartoon suggests that the cartoonist saw x-rays as a force that erased differences.[58] For the specialist, there are a whole range of differences to be considered in an x-ray image, be it gender, age, race, nutrition, and so on. For the public, on the other hand, I believe that the anonymous chest x-ray has a tendency to suggest something humanly real without differentiating it socially, culturally or historically.[59]

Let me contrast this to photography: I have already suggested that both photography and x-ray images are genuine indexes; they

---

[57] *Judge* 32 (1897), cf Knight 1986, p.17. Cf. also Cartwright 1995, p.120; Eisenberg, p.589.

[58] cf Cartwright 1995, p.120.

[59] Cf. also Carthwright 1995, p.107, as to the x-ray image as a metaphorical site stripped of gender and race.

refer to particular objects at specific places at a determinate moment in time; they are datable. In practice, x-ray images are probably given a date more often than photographs. But the point here is not whether or not the image is actually given a date. Neither is it a practical matter (a question of whether or not we are able to decide the date of production for a particular image, or any other object for that matter). The question here is whether or not the image is made part of a socially and culturally constituted calendar, that is, part of the social and cultural history of human beings.

Although there exist historical exceptions to the rule, normally x-ray images seem to be considered to be too *private* or too generic to the human *race* to be experienced as part of our socially stratified, culturally divided and historically changing empirical reality. Let me give some examples:

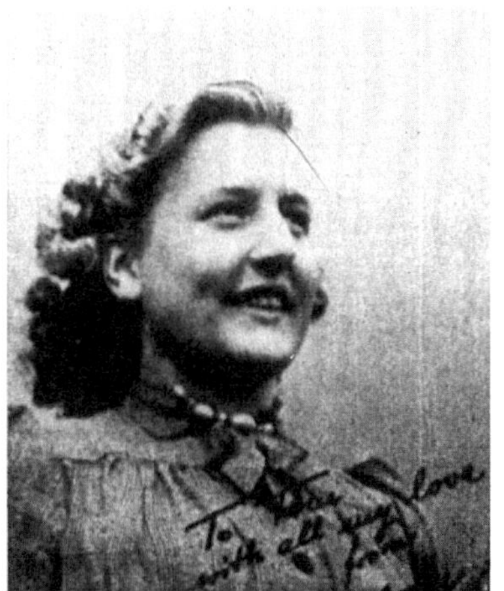

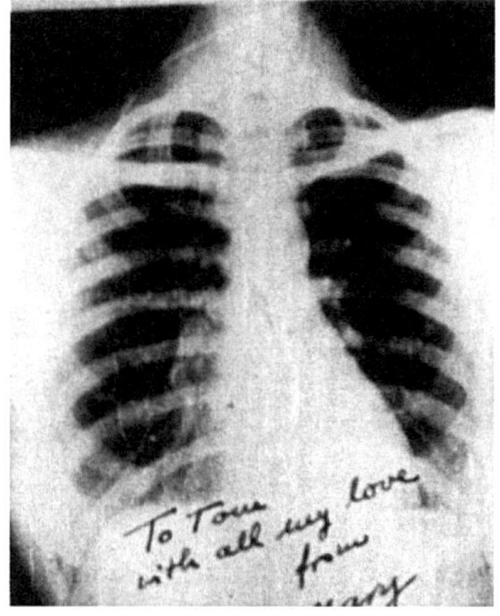

Figure 4. From *Mass Radiography* (1944).

This is a double portrait from a 1944 British government instructional film that teaches industrial managers and workers about the benefits of mass radiography. It is a double portrait of a young woman called Mary, allegedly sent to her boy friend Tom with the same handwritten message on both images: "To Tom, with all my love, from Mary".[60]

In the novel *The Magic Mountain* (1924), Thomas Mann presents a similar idea by letting his main character, Hans Castorp, keep the

[60] cf. Cartwright 1995, p.157.

chest x-ray of his beloved Clavdia in his breast pocket. The image does not mean anything to her, but to Hans Castorp it signifies that she has now put her intimate self into his hands.[61]

The intimacy of these two examples may be surprising, and the romantic attitude towards these particular x-ray images is in no way representative. But they suggest a very *private* dimension to x-ray imaging. Many people would not like to expose this private and even unknown part of themselves. Others seem to have no sense of shame, like Homer Simpson here, who would probably be proud of the distribution of the x-ray image of his diminutive brain.

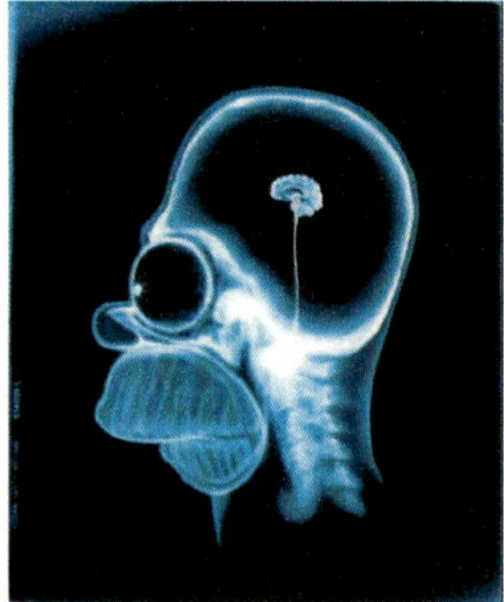

Figure 5. Homer Simpson's brain.

The date given to an x-ray image may be of importance for the individual's medical history. In rare cases, it may also be of importance in a more general but specialised history of medicine. But it is only in exceptional and strongly symbolic cases like the x-ray image of Mrs Röntgen's hand and the x-rayed silhouettes of the dead in the ruins of Hiroshima that x-ray images seem to be recorded in the sociocultural calendar.

Photography is quite different from the x-ray image in this respect. I am not talking about culturally important photographic pictures that are included in our more or less common cultural heritage. I am still talking about whether the datability of the image make it part of our empirical reality. Whereas photographs generally speaking point towards the visible world and are normally thought of as images displaying physical objects from a differentiated empirical world, the x-ray image points towards (private) particularities and

[61] Cf. Mann [1924] 1969, p.348. Cf also van Dijck 2005, p.91.

(anonymous) generalities. The private x-ray image is distributed only in narrow circles and represents a certain resistance to an aesthetic gaze. The anonymous x-ray image, on the other hand, is more in line with what is suggested by the 1897 cartoon above: the non-specialist is not able to judge whether the skeleton displayed by the image is male or female, black or white, rich or poor: it is an image of the human skeleton stripped of time and place, possibly made while the human individual posing for "the x-ray camera" was alive, that is an image of the general (or generic), living, mortal individual.

Compared with the everyday gaze towards photographs, which regardless of the motif has a tendency to neglect the pictorialness of the picture, the normal, uninstructed gaze towards the x-ray image tends to do quite the opposite: the picture as such is very hard to neglect. This is particularly the case for the anonymous, medical x-ray image, referring to a hidden world of bodily mysteries without the personal threat of the potential of an unidentified corporal defect. It appears an image of a human being, like me, as me, naked to the bone, without any marked differences. It is a black and white image of a simplified interior space without the bloody and messy multiplicity of colours and textures. The image is also hazy and extremely flat. Any picture is a visual display on a more or less flat surface. However, in contrast to photographs, which visualise surfaces of objects in space on such a flat surface, the x-ray image visualises the space inside a body in two dimensions on that flat surface. Radiography contains information from the whole depth of the subject, from the ribs through the spine on the chest x-ray. This means that all the internal features of the x-rayed body are superimposed on top of one other.[62] The image may look crisp and clear for the radiologist who is able to identify details in the image and imagine the depth of the body. For the untrained eye, on the other hand, the chest x-ray presents layers of grey shade.

In the chest x-ray, these layers of grey shade form a human figure as they are also formed by a human figure. In contrast to the aesthetics of the microscopic and sub-microscopic world revealing the hidden beauty of balance, structures and relations in living micro-organisms,[63]

---

[62] Cf. for instance Wolbarst 1999.

[63] Cf the 1914 classic book on the subject, *The curves of life*, by Theodore Andrea Cook. Cf also the French physicist Jean Jacques Trillat (1970) and the British artist Gwyneth Thurgood (1971) on how this aesthetics of the natural forms of microorganisms has inspired so-called abstract art and furnishing fabrics.

it forms a human figure: the aesthetics of the chest x-ray is also a matter of scale; one of the key characteristics of radiography is that it produces life size images. The figure displayed is recognisable as humanly real. However, in contrast to the aesthetics of modern art inspired by x-ray technology [64], the chest x-ray does not only depict a transparent human figure. It is also formed by a human figure. The aesthetics of the chest x-ray is a matter of former bodily presence. Whereas the transparency of the handbag through the security screening may stimulate the curiosity of fellow passengers, the transparency of the body displayed in the chest x-ray may rather give life to the experience of vulnerability for both the invading gaze and the danger involved in the x-ray exposure. This vulnerability is not intrusive as long as the anonymous chest x-ray does not demonstrate individual suffering. Individual suffering threatens the aesthetic gaze. The anonymous chest x-ray, on the other hand, seems to stimulate a particular aesthetic engagement with the general, human other. The aesthetics of the chest x-ray is an aesthetic of human vulnerability. Historically we can say that the x-ray image was spontaneously identified with death, before it gradually and in Kevles' words became associated with "good health, with fitting shoes and being told that you did not have tuberculosis" between the world wars.[65] This image is nevertheless even today associated with mortality, not as a shock, but as a human condition. The chest x-ray may appear as particularly illustrative considering its symbolic strength related to the heart and lungs: it is a clean image of general human life, mortal and otherwise vulnerable. The ordinariness of the x-ray image is still part of the public experience even with a high awareness of the risk involved and with competing image technologies knocking at the door, generally more expensive than the old x-ray, less used in most countries and less available to the poor. Even if x-ray technology may be thought of as the medical imaging technology of the last century, it will be used in years to come not only because it is sensitive and specific for certain medical conditions, but also because of its low cost. In every comparison of benefits versus risks and costs, the poor seem to lose. This may add to the appearance of the chest x-ray as an aesthetic of vulnerability.

---

[64] Cf. the studies of Henderson, 1988, 1989 and 2002.
[65] Kevles 1997, p.124.

References

Allen Neil Walsh and Joel Snyder 1975, "Photography, Vision, and Representation", in *Critical Inquiry*, Vol.2, No.1, Autumn 1975, pp.143–169.

Badash, Lawrence 1979, *Radioactivity in America. Growth and Decay of a Science*, John Hopkins UP, Baltimore and London.

Cartwright, Lisa 1995, *Screening the Body. Tracing Medicine's Visual Culture*, University of Minnesota Press.

Clarke, Bruce and Henderson, Linda Dalrymple (eds.) 2002, *From energy to information: representation in science and technology, art, and literature,* Stanford, Calif.: Stanford University Press.

Cheroux, Clement et.al. 2005, *The Perfect Medium: Photography and the Occult*, Yale University Press.

Cook, Theodore Andrea (1914) 1978, *The curves of life*, Dover Publications.

Crary, Jonathan 1988, "Techniques of the observer", *October*, Vol.45 (Summer, 1988), pp.3–35.

Duffin, Jacalyn and Charles R.R.Hayter 2000, "Baring the Sole: The Rise and Fall of the Shoe-Fitting Fluoroscope", in *Iris*, Vol.91, No.2, (Jun.2000), pp.260–282).

Eisenberg, Ronald L. 1992, *RADIOLOGY. An Illustrated History*, Mosby Year Book.

Farmelo, Graham 1995, "The Discovery of X-rays", *Scientific American,* vol.75, No.5, November 1995, pp.86–91.

Glasser, Otto 1993, *Wilhelm Conrad Röntgen and the Early Histoy of the Roentgen Rays*, Norman Publishing; San Francisco.

Grove, Allen W. 1997, "Röntgen's Ghosts: Photography, X-Rays, and the Victorian Imagination", in *Literature and Medicine* 16, (Fall 1997), pp.141–173, John Hopkins University Press.

Halpern, Sydney A. 1992, "Dynamics of Professional Control: Internal Coalitions and Crossprofessional Boundaries", in *The American Journal of Sociology*, Vol.97, No.4, New Directions in the Sociology of Medicine, (Jan.1992), pp.994–1021.

Hady Sy, http://www.ecfa.com/site/artists.php?aid=109 [last chek-ked January 23, 2007]

Hady Sy, http://www.hadysy.com/ [last checked January 23, 2007]

Henderson, Linda Dalrymple 1988, "X Rays and the Quest for Inisible Reality in the Art of Kupka, Duchamp, and the

Cubists", in *Art Journal*, Vol.47, Revising Cubism (Winter 1988), pp.323–340.

Henderson, Linda Dalrymple 1989, "Francis Picabia, radiometers, and X-rays in the 1913", in *The Art Bulletin*, Vol.71, No.1 (Mar.1989), pp.114–123.

Henderson, Linda Dalrymple 2002, "Vibratory Modernism: Boccioni, Kupka, and the Ether of Space" (p.126–149), in Clarke, Bruce and Henderson, Linda Dalrymple Henderson (eds.) *From energy to information: representation in science and technology, art, and literature,* Stanford, Calif.: Stanford University Press, 2002.

Hessenbruch, Arne 2000, "Calibration and Work in the X-ray Economy, 1896–1928, *Social Studies of Science*, Vol.30, No.3, (Jun.2000), pp.397–420.

Kevles, Bettyann Holtzmann 1997, *Naked to the Bone. Medical imaging in the twentieth century*, The Sloan technology series, New Brunswick, N.J.: Rutgers University Press.

Knight, Nancy 1986, "'The New Light': X Rays and Medical Futurism", in Corn, Joseph J. (ed.) *Imaging Tomorrow. History, Technology, and the American Future*, pp.10–34, Cambridge, Massachusetts, the MIT Press.

Knorr-Cetina, Karin and Klaus Amann 1990, "Image Dissection in Natural Science Inquiry", in *Science, Technology, & Human Values*, Vol.15, No.3. (Summer 1990), pp.259–283.).

Lerner, Barron H. 1992, "The Perils of x-ray vision", *Perspectives in biology and medicine*, nr. 35, pp.382–397, Chicago: The University of Chicago Press.

Mackay, R. Stuart 1984, *Medical Images and Displays. Comparisons of Nuclear Magnetic Resonance, Ultrasound, X-Rays, and Other Modalities*, John Wiley & Sons.

Mann, Thomas (1924) 1969, *The Magic Mountain*, trans. Helen Tracy Lowe-Porter, N.Y.: Random House. Originally published as *Der Zauberberg*, Fischer Verlag.

McClafferty, Carla Killough 2001, *The Head Bone's Connected to the Neck Bone. The Weird, Wacky, and Wonderful X-Ray*, New York: Farrar, Straus and Giroux.

Mould, Richard F. 1993, *A Century of X-rays and Radioactivity in Medicine. With Emphasis on Photographic Records of the Early Years*, Institute of Physics Publishing, Bristol and Philadelphia.

Mulligan, Michael E. 1997, *Classic radiological signs. An Atlas and history*, New York/London: The Parthenon Publishing Group.

Peirce, Charles Sander 1885, "On the Algebra of Logic: A Contribution to the Philosophy of Notation", W 5:162–3.

Peirce, Charles Sander 1903, "A Syllabus of Certain Topics of Logic", EP 2:274.

Reiser, Stanley Joel 1978, *Medicine and the Reign of Technology*, Cambridge, Cambridge UP.

Saxby, Graham 2002, *The Science of Imaging. An Introduction*, Bristol and Philadelphia, Institute of Physics Publishing (*IoP*).

Seiju Toda 1995, *X = t: the art of X-ray photography*, introduction by Max Kozloff. New York: Hudson Hills Press.

Thomas, Ann 1999, "The Search for Pattern", in Thomas, Ann (ed.) *Beauty of Another Order: Photography in Science*, Yale UP, pp.76–119.

Thurgood, Gwyneth 1971, "On the Artist and Science", in *Leonardo*, Vol.4, No.2 (Spring 1971), pp.117–124.

Trillat, Jean Jacques 1970, "Art, Aesthetics and Physics: The contribution of physics to modern art", in *Leonardo*, Vol.3, No.1 (Jan.1970), pp.47–54.

van Dijck, José 2005, *The Transparent Body. A Cultural Analysis of Medical Imaging*, University of Washington Press.

Wolbarst, Anthony Brinton 1999, *Looking Within. How X-Ray, CT, MRI, Ultrasound, and Other Medical Images Are Created and How They Help Physicians Save Lives*, University of California Press.

Ina Blom

Lamps, Television and Biopolitics

Moments towards an alternative history of the avant-garde media art

> A chandelier hangs from the ceiling of what will be a living room, a bed light stands on the floor of what will be a bedroom. Lights are on in all the rooms. To start with, it was a sales gimmick: with light falling fast, it was decided to put lights in the rooms to give an impression of life as people walked around the housing complex.[1]

I

Consider a strange media object: a film that is nothing but its own scenario – that is, a generative point of departure for the production of film itself. Consider, then, that this scenario primarily presents itself in spatial terms: it is a building. But not your typical kind of building: this particular building is primarily a lamp – a strange tent-like structure covered with semi-transparent elastomer sheets that lights up at night like a giant Noguchi lamp (the sheet material diffuses light in the same way as a decorative living room lamp). Placed among rice fields in Chiang Mai in Thailand, the inside of this lamp-building is simply a dynamo calibrated to generate electricity for ten light bulbs thanks to the raw muscle power of local water buffalo pulling a two-ton steel counterweight. The lamp building then extracts biopower in the most obvious sense of the term.[2]

This lamp building has no other function than that of serving as the scenario for a film: like all film scenarios it previews or "projects"

---

[1] Huyghe, Pierre, and Parreno, Philippe, "The Story of a Feeling (Notes)" in *Dominique Gonzales-Foerster, Pierre Huyghe, Philippe Parreno.* Exhibitions catalogue, Musée d'art Moderne de la Ville de Paris, 1999, p. 116.

[2] The structure, named *Hybrid Muscle*, was produced by the architectural company Roche & Cie in 2002. The original plan was to use the muscle power of an elephant – an important element in the Thai tourist industry.

narrative material for a potential film. But in this case it would be more correct to say that it is not the film narrative, but the luminous film projection itself that is being previewed or projected. It is as if the lamp building already imagines the light that the film itself will generate – or more precisely, the glowing, atmospheric surround of the film screening, a surround that could obviously also be considered an inhabited space. The luminous space that normally serves only to *diffuse* or distribute a pre-existing narrative is – in this case – already present *as* the "narrative" material of this particular film.[3]

The film is called *The Boy from Mars,* a title that promises a science fiction story. But the only "story" that unfolds in *The Boy from Mars* is simply the lighting of the glowing lamp building as darkness falls over the rice fields, and the buffalo do their work. Daytime shots give us a more precise idea of the structure of the lamp building and the workings of its muscle-powered dynamo. At this point the structure looks quite mundane: wind and rain tear at its elastomer skin. But then darkness falls, the lamp

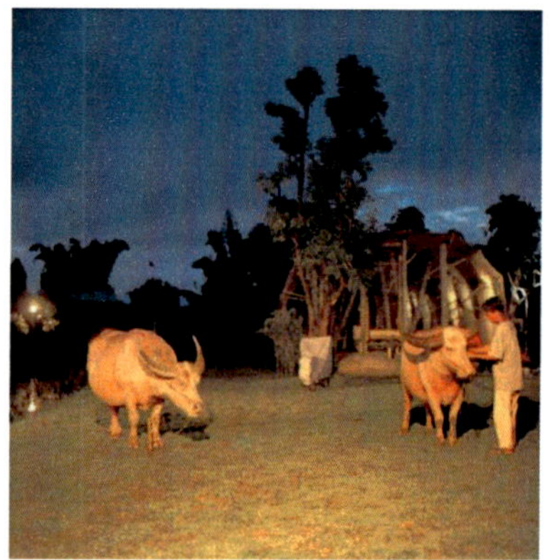

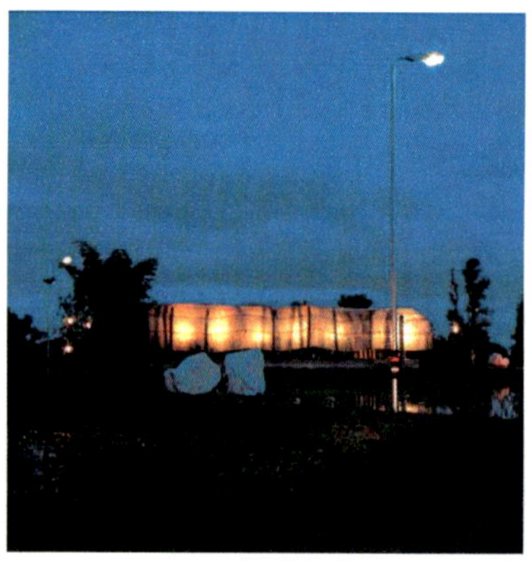

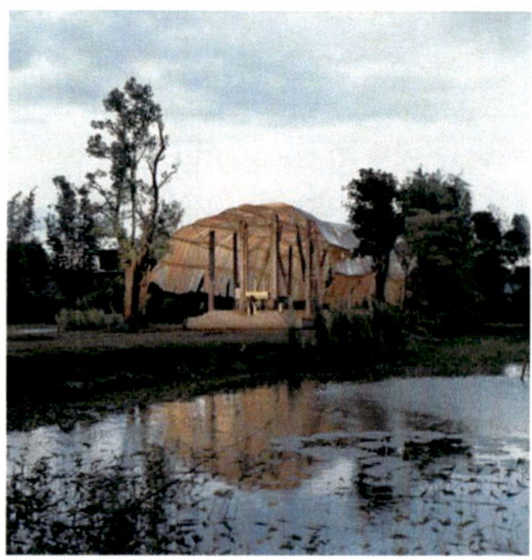

Figure 1-3. Philippe Parreno, 3 stills from *The Boy from Mars*, 35mm film, 2003.

[3] It should of course be noted here that in French the word *diffusion* is, in many contexts, synonymous with *distribution.*

lights up again and the projective magic of the scenario mentality is restored. For projection – whether described as subjective fantasy, mental prevision of the future, cinema screening or encounters with alien worlds – notably tends to be imagined in terms of the cone of light that cuts through the darkness of night. When the romantic tradition takes on the lamp (rather than the mirror) as the central metaphor for artistic production, the lamp indicates precisely a projective aesthetics in which the mind so to speak lights up or shapes reality.[4] In contrast to the artistic ideals associated with the mirror metaphor (idealist or realist representations of the existing world), the cone of light that cuts through darkness is associated with becoming, with the futurist modes of thinking and creation that would mark modernity. And, one could add, with the media machines that would be intimately associated with modern art production and its projective imagination.

The few obvious science fiction elements in *The Boy from Mars* therefore emerge only as if in extension of this projective lamplight. In the darkness of the night landscape, the lamp building seems associated with three other sources of light: the few street lamps that exist in the area, the moon that appears behind drifting skies, and a series of star-like lights that move slowly across the night sky and that we soon recognise as some kind of alien visitation. In a scene that presents itself like a classic sci-fi representation, the lone buffalo in the night field is the only observer of these UFOs. The point, however, is that the most evident traces of the sci-fi narrative promised in the film's title only appear as if an afterthought to the presentation of projective media machinery. This media machinery appears to us under two guises. On the one hand it is an entirely comprehensible technical structure: a muscle powered electrical generator. On the other hand it is a slowly unfolding luminous and atmospheric presence filled with untold potential: a generator that draws not on muscle power but on the power of thinking and imagination.

This is, one could argue, the specific form of biopower that is extracted in modern media machines in general. And from this perspective *The Boy from Mars* could be seen as one of a long series of recent artworks in which the power of thinking or the power of

---

[4] Abrams, M.H., *The Mirror and the Lamp. Romantic Theory and the Critical Tradition,* Oxford University Press 1971. The mirror metaphor of artistic production notably indicates the ability of the artwork to deliver a mimetic representation (idealist or realist) of the world.

affects are emphatically associated with the workings of the media and information machines, rather than with whatever type of humanistic content that might be seen to pass through the production and distribution apparatuses of such media. In order to bring out the implications of this perspective as a concrete material structure open for experience and for thinking, the work in question tends to reverse, or to radically reconfigure, the habitual production logic of media such as film and TV.

As expressions of what Deleuze and Guattari would call the larger "social machines", media technologies like film and TV are production apparatuses that draw on the flexible, diversified and subjective imaginations of the new future that are essential to the expansive dynamics of contemporary capitalism.[5] Going beyond the controlled production of newness associated with the older planning economies (a new always carefully based on the parameters of the known), today's production of newness is vested in the ability to capitalise on the suggested *potential* of a number of hypothetical futures. Sometimes dubbed "the scenario mentality", its driving force is not a planning committee disciplining the future to take place according to a desired pattern, but media machines that create social spaces and forms of subjectivation where individual cognitive activity is aligned with the dynamics of capital interests. Yet, in general, film and TV disguise their role as the privileged technologies of the new scenario mentality. This disguise is possible because the projection of hypothetical futures is usually identified with a narrative structure (for instance a science fiction novel) that is seen as *previous to* – and thus also fundamentally independent of – the media machines in which they are presented. Everything then proceeds as if the fantasy of the future just happened to pass through the apparatus of film or television. The feature film or the TV series is simply presented as the end product of a narrative desire whose origins lay elsewhere: putatively in the autonomous imaginative capacities of human (artistic) consciousness.

Philippe Parreno's film turns this logic on its head. The subject matter of this film, whose title indicates a typical sci-fi narrative, is nothing *but* a scenario – an emerging or endlessly generative *place*

---

[5] The concept of social machines is launched in Deleuze, Gilles and Guattari, Felix, *Anti-Oedipus,* translated by Robert Hurley, Mark Seem and Helen R. Lane, London: Athlone Press, 1984.

of production for the cinematic projection itself. But what is really essential here is that this place of production primarily emerges in spatial and atmospheric terms, as a building, or an inhabitable surround. This is a strategy that is pursued in other works by Parreno: *Mount Analogue,* a video film that consists only of changing colour emanations is screened inside an apartment in Paris, so that the film lights up both the apartment and – through its windows – the night streets outside. Again, it is a case of a film functioning as a lamp. The durations and rhythms of the luminous colour changes are the end products of a complex media process which, again, eschews the use of narrative as an independent point of departure for media production. The colour changes are generated by Morse code signals that beat out the words of a text, a story. But this text is the story *of* a film, a film based on René Daumal's unfinished mystical /spiritual novel *Mount Analogue* (1952). This means that the video light that illuminates the Parisian apartment like a sophisticated mood lamp is the coded expression of a film translated into a narrative, which is in turn coded in one of the languages of information processing. One might say that everything in the work happens within the folds of information and media machines. But this is very emphatically not just a formalist play with the technological supports of aesthetic expressions. The association between lamps, technological media and the question of habitation, traced in work after work, is, in contrast, an aesthetic-political strategy that makes visible the specific ways in which the contemporary media machines should be understood as social sites, sites that represent specific subjectivation processes. It is an artistic strategy that compels one to see these media machines as producers of social relations or social spaces before one sees them as producers of specific aesthetic expressions or ideological messages. By turning media productions into inhabited media spaces, spaces that are more remarkable for their atmospheric qualities than for their presentational focus, this type of work explores the forces at work in the life-environment formed and informed by modern media and the mediatic logic of projection.

II

It seems obvious, then, that the effort to make visible the mediatic production of social space has to be approached in terms of the bodies it modulates and the type of subjectivities it produces.[6] The shift in the ontology of political theory outlined in the later work of Michel Foucault and that was initiated with the concept of biopower – the early modern turn towards a form of government that no longer only ruled on death but occupied itself with the *life* of the population on an increasingly detailed scale – is informative in this context. For this is a political theory that departs from the body and its potential and that regards the political subject as an ethical subject rather than a subject of law: here the aesthetic dimension of existence itself takes on a new political centrality. In the work of Michael Hardt and Antoni Negri, a contemporary form of biopower or biopolitics signals a new era of capitalist production where the borderlines between economics and politics and between production and reproduction are eroding. Life is no longer limited to the domain of reproduction or subordinated to the working process: a new form of social production takes all facets of human life into consideration.[7] It is in the context of this shift to the politics and economics of the subject and its life forces that works like the ones discussed above focus on the specific ways in which bodies and media machines are integrated in the everyday environment (as opposed to, for instance, the critique of media institutions or programming formats performed or articulated in numerous works of art.)

And it is also in the context of this shift that the lamp (re)emerges as a key figure in aesthetic production. Through the figure of the lamp – which must be seen here as a *strategic* device rather than simply an

---

[6] This idea of "making visible" is related to Gilles Deleuze's discussion of the relation between discourses and visibilities. Visibility is here not simply a perceptible thing or quality: it is also a form of knowledge. To see the contours of such forms of knowledge means to find a strategy of seeing what is not immediately apparent to our sight, i.e. to take an interest in the very circumstances under which something becomes part of what is obviously visible. Deleuze, Gilles, *Foucault.* Translated by Sean Hand. University of Minnesota Press, 1988, pp. 47-70.

[7] Hardt, Michael and Negri, Antioni, *Empire,* Cambridge University Press, 2000. The relevant texts by Foucault are *The History of Sexuality, Vol. I. An Introduction.* London: Allen Lane 1979, "Governmentality", in Graham Burchell, Colin Gordon & Peter Miller, *The Foucault Effect: Studies in Governmentality,* Harvester Wheatsheaf 1991, pp. 87-104 and *Society Must Be Defended. Lectures at the Collège de France 1975-76,* New York: Picador 2003. As Thomas Lemke and others have pointed out, it should be noted that the biopolitics outlined by Hardt and Negri is a somewhat narrower term than the one invented by Foucault and which covers subject areas like hygiene, demography, social welfare and insurance systems. (Thomas Lemke, "A Zone of Indistinction. A Critique of Giorgio Agambens Concept of Biopolitics", in *Outlines. Critical Social Studies,* Vol. 7, No. 1, 2005, pp. 3-13).

aesthetic object in its own right – media production is so to speak displaced from the habitual association with specialist technologies and dominant producers of messages and relocated to the "home", or the everyday life environment of individual bodies. In fact, the sheer *amount* of lamp-related works in recent art production, and their regular distribution throughout the field of contemporary art, suggests that the desire to engage with the mediatic production of social relations is not an exotic or exceptional interest found in a few works only, but key to the way in which contemporary art *places itself* in relation to media production in general. For decades, the interaction between art, new media technologies and social production has been a force field that organises the various strategies and expressions of modernist and avant-garde art. But the lamp works may indicate a structural shift in this relation itself. The century-long identification between art and new media can no longer simply be read as a quest for new artistic formats that are in step with an evolving communications culture or as disruptive Situationist-type interventions in hegemonic media. For when media production is literally brought home – home to the spaces of personal sensations, memories and affects – they offer a different perspective on what was at stake in the avant-garde's famous quest to operate in the politically "real", to erase the boundary separating life practice and art practice. Now this quest itself emerges as a corollary to a biopolitical form of production in which all facets of life, and not least those associated with aesthetic experiences and sensations, are rendered politically pertinent and economically productive. The lamp works simply provide a new form of access to the specific body-machine connections that have a privileged place in this economy.

In recent art, the art/life boundary seems to be articulated less through an emphasis on the politics of institutions than on the stylistics of the inhabited environment: the cool or colourful, minimal or crowded surfaces of architecture and design, indoor and outdoor spaces, furniture, fashion. These are spatial practices that exemplify the effort of the scenario mentality to invest the world with projective potentiality: the tourist industry's presentation of the world as a series of precisely framed environments, each with its distinctive "style" or atmosphere, gives us this production of space in its most rudimentary form. And it is within this general set-up that the lamp seems to turn up with surprising frequency – the designer lamps that both decorate and illuminate the everyday. The lamps are all at once tokens of the projective logic that informs the current style and fashion-based economies, metaphorical figures that evoke the romantic idea of the mind and purely technical devices for projecting light. For the lamps in question are really lamps in the most everyday sense of the word – the chandeliers, neon ceiling fixtures and lamp posts that light up homes and offices, public buildings and streets – as opposed to more abstract orchestrations of light effects in (for instance) the work of James Turrell. What they make visible – what they offer up for both sensation and reflection – is, more particularly, the peculiar conditions of perception within contemporary inhabited environments: the hyper-styled environments that are also electrically wired and electronically connected, informed by mediatic and informational processes and procedures. The lamps direct us, in short, to a field of artistic articulation in which art, technology, media, economic production and lifestyles are treated as one continuum. It is a field in which the visual essentially comes to denote "televisual", and where the televisual itself emerges as a productive framework that extends far beyond its typical journalistic and/ or aesthetic formats and forms of programming.

From the laterna magica to the popular idea of TV as the modern fireplace, there is a long history of associating film, TV and video with the basic function of lamps or other sorts of lighting furniture. (In 1950s America, a variety of TV lamps or TV-related lamps were developed, designed to "extend" the mood-light the TV set itself would produce.) The new lamp works operate as if in extension of this historical connection. Rather than approaching media in terms of the particular types of representations they emit, they focus on the way in which live electronic imagery is incorporated into our living spaces and interacts with our daily routines and modes of inhabitation. Once established as a distinct perspective, the association between lamps and television comes to include all the different types of live electronic signals: from the lights of digital clock radios and mobile phones to the constantly flickering advertising messages that illuminate our cities at night. The lamp works then draw on the change in the mediatic function of the home that took place with the invention of electric light. In Marshall McLuhan's cybernetic terminology, electric light is pure information: there is no redundancy and hence no pre-digested content. It is a self-contained communication system in which the medium really is the message, in the sense that it represents a pure capacity for transformation or differentiation. Its most marked achievement is that of framing the world and thereby continually recreating it. Electric light creates visibility where previously there was nothing. It produces spaces without walls, continually redraws the urban landscape and pulls us into the newfound worlds of the sub-microscopic and the subterranean.[8] Out of this perspective arises the widespread notion that contemporary living spaces can also be understood as informational interfaces. And it is along this line of reasoning that a continuity is established between lamplight and TV signals, since both evoke the creative or projective logic of mental operations: both electric light and TV signals seem to light "through" things, rather than lighting "on" things. But what is missing from the cybernetic account of informational media is, as Mark Hansen has pointed out, precisely the way in which the body is always the framer and shaper of the informational realm.[9] Such an embodied perspective is, in contrast, brought to the foreground in the lamp works and their emphasis on the realm of atmospherics.

Work after work then seems to draw the same connection between lamplight, atmospherics and media. On the one hand, there are lamps that hang or stand in exhibition spaces and installations, mysteriously silent, glowing, looking good. They seem to trigger no other impulses than a basic desire to just hang around, to bask in the aura of the lamps. On the other hand, a closer look provides, again and again, the same association between lamps, real-time media and the omnipresence of electronic networks. Cerith Wyn Evans's elaborate crystal chandeliers hang adjacent to computer screens showing a program that transforms informational material into Morse code signals: these signals in turn control the distribution of lamplight. Pierre Huyghe's grid-like ceiling lamp can be played like an Atari computer game and Angela Bulloch's light grid boxes and walls

---

[8] McLuhan, Marshall: *Understanding Media. The Extensions of Man,* The MIT Press, 1994, pp. 7-22 and 123-131.

[9] Hansen, Mark, *New Philosophy for New Media,* MIT Press, 2006. A key point in Hansen's analysis is his attempt to historicise the post-human view that is central to the science of Cybernetics. This view evolves out of the Shannon-Weaver theory of information, that views information in stochastic or probabilistic terms: the key issue in their information theory was not the communication of significance or meaning but the optimisation of the signal-to-noise ratio in message transmission. Alternative accounts of information, such as the one developed by Donald McKay, also takes interpretation into account as part of the structural component of message: information is defined in terms of the mutual constitution of message and receiver. This model was dropped by American cybernetics.

function like giant pixel screens. The light from Olafur Eliasson's projector lamps often mime the visual effects of video projection, while a project currently under development presents spherical lamps that are actually reconstructed TV sets: their continually changing light flows consist of informational material from whatever TV-channel the lamp is tuned in to.[10]

Then there are lamps whose glowing presence is even more "essentially" televisual, in the sense that it literally transmits other times and places. The pretty glass lamps that Tobias Rehberger installed in the medieval tunnels in the Italian city of San Gimignano did not simply facilitate perception of the place itself: thanks to a computer program and an internet connection they gave off a quantity of light that would at any given moment correspond to the actual quantity of sunlight in the South American city of Montevideo. (The choice of the city of Montevideo was in fact a direct function of its "televisual" name). But the atmospheric continuity between lamps and real-time media – the sensation of the home environment as interface – is perhaps nowhere as clearly articulated as in the interiors of Dominique Gonzales-Foerster, that seem to explore the way in which the great cinematic spaces are in fact integrated into the home itself. This intimate relation with the expansive media environment is also explored in a series of non-narrative video films that seem to highlight the very presence of the spectator (ordinarily placed at the margin of the cinematic apparatus, hidden in the dark cinema space) by functioning as luminous and atmospheric surrounds rather than simply as screen works to be watched. While traditional cinema places the viewer at the margin of the cinematic apparatus, hidden in the dark, never interfering with the cone of light, Gonzales Foerster's film illuminates the viewer, at the same time as the viewer frames and mobilises the cinematic material. These are films that work *as* lamps: as they document atmospheric spaces around the world, glowing tourist dreamscapes that testify to the projective shaping and selling of the world, they also present themselves as atmosphere-producers in their own right. This mode of presentation reaches an extreme in Gonzales Forester's *Ipanema Theories* – a film whose image-material moves from lamp to lamp throughout the 90 minutes of its duration,

[10] The individual light points that makes up the TV screen is here distributed on a spherical construction. For this reason, no coherent TV image is transmitted, only light signals of changing colors.

as if caught in a particularly hypnotic confusion of the basic tenets of film projection and its documentary content.

III

A discussion of the integration of bodies and media machines brought into focus by the lamp works would then above all seem to need a critical concept of the atmospheric, and a more precise idea of how such a concept could relate to mediatic situations. Despite the extensive focus on spatiality in the art of the last half-century – on social spaces as well as natural spaces – the concept of the atmospheric has not been part of the vocabulary of art-critical discourse or aesthetic theory. The one place in which the notion of atmospheres seems to have found some sort of grounding is in a contemporary musical discourse preoccupied with the spatial continuity of material sounds or frequencies evoked in so-called ambient music. In his attempts to describe music as an environmental or ecological system, a dynamic and all-encompassing world designed for inhabitation and living, David Toop refers to the philosopher Gernot Böhme, who uses the idea of atmospheres as a point of departure for a new environmentalist philosophy that pays attention to the more elusive aspects of our experience of the environment. Atmospheres are here understood as in-between phenomena that stand between subjects and objects: while they always refer back to subjective perception, they are also object-like emotions that are so to speak cast into a shared space. A potential link to a conceptual framework that takes the mediatic environment into account emerges as Böhme presents Walter Benjamin as a theorist of atmospheres. For the concept of the aura – the experience of the unique, if distant presence of the original work of art (that seems lost in the modern media reality) – contains a hidden theory of the atmospheric impact of aesthetic experience, at least if one is to take Benjamin's actual examples of the auratic experience seriously. The key reference here is of course Benjamin's description of a person resting outdoors on a summer day and who is so to speak "breathing" the aura of the natural phenomena around him. To Böhme, Benjamin describes a way of inhabiting aesthetic experiences that may be an apt explanation of the effects of great works of art, but that is certainly not exclusive to them. For we inhabit other "things" aesthetically as well – a fact that becomes clearer to us once we leave behind the classical thing-ontology and instead pay attention to "the ecstasy of things" – that is how things appear for our sensory register.[11]

This observation would be all the more relevant if Benjamin's essay were simply a theory of aesthetic experience. But the fact is that Böhme's analysis, which somehow puts Benjamin's preoccupation with the changed status of the work of art in parenthesis, then also neglects its all-important historical perspective. For Benjamin discusses art mainly in order to focus on the implications of a crucial change in the mode of economic production – a type of focus that gives a far more precise notion of how we live in our modern media environments than what the more general or ahistorical concept of atmospheres can provide. In Benjamin's writing, the work of art associated with the "atmospheric" concept of aura seems to serve as a *strategic tool* that puts a historically new relationship between production and perception into sharp relief. And this strategy may be directly relevant to understanding the peculiar use of lamps and lamp-related objects in recent art. What Benjamin's essay describes is thus not so much the general disappearance of the aura of the original work of art. It deals, more poignantly, with the complex question of the *return* of the aura under the radically changed conditions of production that characterise the modern media and leisure industries. For the auratic or "atmospheric" form of "distant presence" is not simply lost in modern media environments. Benjamin's theory suggests, on the contrary, that a different form of aesthetic inhabitation of spaces takes place under these conditions.

The idea of the return of the aura has been described in some detail by Samuel Weber, who claims that Benjamin's understanding of the aura (the distant presence of original artworks) actually corresponds with the particular modes of presentation provided by modern mass media. It corresponds, in particular, to the specific perceptual situation produced through TV's live transmissions, its real-time flow of signals. For, in contrast to film and photography, which provide representations of different or distant times and places, television provides a medial set-up in which perception itself is experienced in its differentiation. Its live transmissions do not simply overcome distance, but seem to somehow short-circuit the

---

[11] Böhme, Gernot, *Atmosphäre. Essays zur neuen Ästhetik.* Suhrkamp Verlag, Frankfurt 1995.

notion of distance itself. It renders distance invisible by transposing it directly into the vision it transmits. This short-circuiting implies a radical separation that splits the unity of the body's time and space – a well-known feature of both film and photography as well. But in television this separation is combined with a *presentness* associated with sense perception that involves the actuality of the body in a very different way. It sets up a surrogate for the body in that it allows sense perception to take place, but in a way no body can, for its perception takes place in more than one place at a time. In contrast to film and photography, television (with its live events and real-time transmissions) does not transmit images or representations, but the semblance of presentation as such.[12]

So, what disappears in the age of mechanical reproduction is not aura as such, but the aura of art as the *work* of representation, a work that would have its fixed place, that would take its place as a "world-picture". Here, Weber contrasts Benjamin's thinking with Heidegger's dystopian idea of the world-picture – the schematic and universalising *representation* of the world that is produced in the new realm of global media technology. Or, to be more precise, he identifies Benjamin's idea of the return of auratic images with the few hints that Heidegger gives of possible openings or escape-routes out of the world picture. Heidegger describes such escape-routes through metaphors of light and shadow: if the world picture is a zone of light, a system of visibility where everything has its fixed place, this system's difference can only be a shadow. "Shadow" here signifies not a lack of light but simply what escapes representation: the shadow, which "bears witness to an always concealed glow", is a differentiating agent in the sense that it constitutes an "other" production of light, a form of visibility that continually differentiates itself from the matrix of the world-picture. [13]

This again makes it possible to describe the aura that returns in the new mediascape – the transient and ephemeral, close-up yet always distant images of television – as "bright shadows": They produce glowing appearances, ambiences, or atmospheres that speak of a flexible modulation of the very perception of presence. The new medial order, and the mode of production that goes with it, make

---

[12] Weber, Samuel, *Mass Mediauras: Form, Technics, Media,* Stanford University Press 1996, pp. 76 – 129.

[13] Weber, op.cit, pp. 76 -86.

it evident that the type of perception associated with auratic phenomena can now only be understood *as an event*, and that it bestows an event-like quality on the bodies that align their perceptual and sensory register with its technological apparatus.[14] The essay on art in the age of mechanical reproduction primarily deals with this issue through an analysis of film. But the aspects of film mentioned by Benjamin actually point forward to conditions that are, in a more fundamental way, characteristic of the medium of television. His preoccupation seems less focused on filmic representation than with the process of recording: the event-like blink of the camera-eye and the strange temporal continuity between recording and real life, demonstrated by the cameraman who records images at the same speed as the speed of people talking. This is a type of focus that is characteristic of live TV or real-time video and that would be crucially important in the early developments of so-called television or video art. The return of the aura is then essentially a question of the deep and intimate way in which television connects itself to the perceptual processes of human bodies.[15]

IV

The question of how television engages perception then also emerges as a key issue in any attempt to understand power formation in the age of television. Here, the habitual preoccupation with the content of TV messages is an insufficient explanatory framework, since it tends to only explain the interpellation of subjects to specific ideological representations or "world pictures". TV's far more flexible modulation of perceptions and affects remains hidden from view, along with the specific type of politics that it serves.[16] In going beyond the level of the TV message, one must, as Serge Daney

---

[14] Weber, op.cit, pp. 86 -88.

[15] Benjamin, Walter *Das Kunstwerk im Zeitalter seiner Technischen Reprodusierbarkeit*, Frankfurt/Main: Suhrkamp, 1963.

[16] Félix Guattari presents an alternative to Louis Althusser's influential notion of ideological state apparatuses: Media machineries are in his view not frameworks that secure the reproduction of ideology through the mechanism of interpellation but, rather, frameworks that reproduce the mediums of production and productive relations. This point is discussed in Maurizio Lazzarato, *Videophilosophie, Zeitwahrnähmung im Postfordismus,* B-Books, Berlin: 2002, pp. 129-156. The relevant text by Guattari is *La Révolution Moléculaire,* 10/18, Paris 1977.

pointed out, cease to see TV as one definable "thing", or – in this case, as one definable medium. Instead we must reconstruct its mode of functioning through different categories and frameworks than the ones we normally use.[17] One must, in other words, temporarily forget about the two major frameworks that inform our understanding of televisual images: the typical propaganda machine of the classical mass medium *or* a purely aesthetic framework in which mass media technologies are deployed for different purposes (the production of video art). The interdependence between these two traditional ways of understanding televisual imagery can be seen in the desire, expressed by many artists and critics in the 1960s and 70s, to use the propaganda-machine of television for a wider distribution of video art. Such perspectives basically reflect a legalistic concern with the freedom or lack of freedom, the visibility or lack of visibility, of art objects within the dominant sphere of mass media.

Yet, the earliest artistic experiments with television and video technologies constituted a practice in which television was systematically inscribed in a wider grid of relations.[18] These experiments served the needs and interests of an avant-garde art that understood its own productions as a form of activism that operated beyond the boundaries of specific artistic media and genres, and in the critical interface between art systems and life processes. Early TV artists thus remained in a curious outsider/ observer position vis-à-vis the medium they had chosen to work with. Unlike most art-oriented filmmakers, they did not simply learn to work with a technology or a medium in the more limited sense of the word. From their outsider

---

[17] Daney, quoted in Lazzarato, op.cit. p.82.

[18] As Dieter Daniels has pointed out, the art practices that grew out of the TV medium differed in significant ways from the type of artistic practices that grew out of film, photography and radio. In all three cases, the medium developed its own properly artistic forms of expression – forms that helped nurture utopian dreams of an integration of art and mass culture. Dreams of a televisual medium not yet created also informed some avant-garde projects and writings. But an actual *artistic* experimentation with televisual techniques only took place once television was established as the world's dominant mass medium, and recognised (by artists and theorists alike) as a prime instrument of the culture industry. And, significantly, these artistic experiments were never identified or promoted as "television art" by the official medium of television (in the way the film industry would recognize the more solipsistic "artistic" productions as part of its *own* range of expressions). For this reason, TV or video art passed completely outside the production and distribution circuits of TV. Daniels, Dieter, *Kunst als Sendung, Von der Telegraphie zum Internet*, München: Verlag C.H. Beck, 2002, 241-249.

position they seemed, from day one, to enter into a highly explicit dialogue with a whole set of institutional, cultural or economic practices. TV was not so much a medium of expression as a cultural and economic *fact*. It could, in other words, not be dealt with without taking into account its mode of functioning within larger cultural and economic contexts. For this reason, early TV or video artworks seemed to present highly self-reflexive observations on the complicity between the medium of TV and "creative" production in a wider economic sense of the word. In fact, the more traditional understanding of "video art" as a properly artistic *medium* and a series of genre conventions – integrated not into the mass media system but into the system of contemporary visual art – was a later development.

In early video art, the television screen was therefore systematically integrated into larger environmental, atmospheric or interactive set-ups – a sign that right from the outset a concern with the connection between the real-time flow of signals and ideas about mediatic "life production" holds centre stage. In fact, a "video-philosophy" devoted to the question of the wider grid of mediatic relations was developed in embryonic and fragmented form in the writings, instructions and manifests of video art pioneer Nam June Paik. A key point in this work was his focus on video as a time dispenser, a medium that, above all, produces and manipulates time. But time here is not approached in the abstract, as is often the case in the type of critical argument that promotes temporality and indeterminacy in the arts over the more static art forms. In Paik's work and writings, time is above all treated as a singularly important *economic* factor, a valuable commodity that is explicitly compared to an energy source like oil. But the perspectives outlined in his work and writing were subsequently largely forgotten – probably because of the way in which video technology primarily seemed to provide the basis for a new artistic medium that allowed a visual documentation of the contingent, the personal and the intimately day-to-day. But recently Paik's fragmented video-philosophy has re-emerged in a far more comprehensive and detailed form in the writings of Italian philosopher Maurizio Lazzarato, who sees video as a general framework for understanding contemporary social relations. In his view, the specific time processing or time production in video technology closely mimics the processes of thinking and memory, and this proximity with mental processes makes TV and video the ideal machinery for a form of production that is often named "cognitive capitalism" or "information economy". "Video-philosophy" is then mainly a way of seeing the main product of this economy – notably the production of subjectivity.[19]

The point of departure for Lazzarato's hypothesis is the following analysis: in post-industrial (or post-Fordian) economies, value is no longer mainly accrued from factory work or production in the workplace. Now all aspects of our lives – from our work time to our so-called free time down to the level of our cognitive operations, our thinking, affects and sensibilities – have become economically productive. And to the extent that cognitive operations are what "gives" or "produces" any notion of temporality, one could say that time itself is subject to the capitalist creation of value. If TV and video are part of a group of technologies that primarily seems to work on and with temporality itself, there may be a fundamental complicity between such technologies and cognitive operations – as well as with contemporary economic production. The framework for this analysis is Henri Bergson's model for understanding time: TV and video technologies may be called time crystallisation technologies since their capacity for condensing, extending, recapitulating and previewing time closely resembles the way the mind itself deals with temporality. Time, here, is not a linear process, but a crystallisation of past, present and future. The present is conserved in the memory of the past and the past is a memory of the contemporary. In *Matter and Memory*, Bergson presents a model for a non-psychological memory – a sort of ontological memory that could also be called a virtual memory, in the sense that the coexistence of the present and the past described through the concept of time crystallisation is a coexistence of the actual and the virtual.[20] TV technology can of course only imitate the complexities of memory in a very limited way, but what it *can* do is to reproduce its temporalities: TV presents or memorises the past within the productive presence of a real-time flow that inserts a split in the presence of the viewing body itself. Through their particular ways of storing and distributing time, TV or video technologies then actually function like a form of social memory: as they store and manipulate time, they work alongside the mental processes of thought or intellectual work in general.

---

[19] Lazzarato, Maurizio op.cit.

[20] Bergson, Henri *Matter and Memory*, Translated by N.M. Paul and W.S. Palmer, New York: Zone Books 1991.

This point is reinforced if Bergson's description of the workings of perception is compared with how video technologies handle what is commonly referred to as "images". Bergson imagines perception as a sort of interaction with flows or streams of images that create relations between various forms and types of durations. Images are then not phenomena that spring out of subjective imagination or even out of human activity: they exist outside and beyond such activity as autonomous phenomena, i.e. as streams of light. Human activity creates its own particular cuts or intersections in these streams and in this way establishes a relation between signifying and a-signifying streams – i.e. between meaningful visual durations and random streams of light. The crucial point here is that – in contrast to other time-based visual media, such as film and photography – video and digital technologies distinguish themselves by operating along exactly the same "perceptual" logic. As Paik has pointed out, there is no such thing as an "image-space" in a television image. Television images consist of continually moving flows of light: the flows are both recorded and processed, and can therefore never be contained as spatial unities the way a still photography seems to "contain" a certain spatial continuity. Spatial information is translated into points and lines that have no spatial extension. The mode of extension of video images is purely temporal: video is nothing but a modulation of time. In relation to TV, the world is always already an image: there is no longer any question of representing or making images, but of manipulating images. Video technology gives us access to something that belongs to the realm of pure perception as it interacts with, or creates various forms of durations or cuts within, the streams of light or image-flows that exist independently of this particular technology or medium.[21] The affective power of these technologies (which may be seen in our readiness to make them into prosthetic devices for our bodies and environments) comes precisely from this ability to replicate the very *force and activity* of pulling together and spreading out time – a force and an activity that approaches that of intellectual work itself. Since, according to Nietzsche, thinking and perception represent affects, or forms of the will to power, technologies that resemble thinking and perception will then also replicate this affective dimension to thinking.

---

[21] Lazzarato, op.cit., pp. 65-89.

However, technologies cannot be thought of in a social vacuum, and if time and its affects are being reproduced in contemporary technological machines, it is only because these machines replicate or express the coupling between capitalist production and cognitive operations in today's "social machines". Contemporary time crystallisation technologies are obviously not the first technologies to demonstrate a specific relationship to time. But while earlier thermodynamic technologies would crystallise *time in general*, the newer machines crystallise the durations within perception, sensation and thinking.[22] In this sense, the omnipresence of video technologies is an index of our fundamental subjection to a type of production that capitalises on thought itself or affective power – a new and powerful non-organic form of energy. They extract a form of power that we may, in simpler terms, call *attention*: recent writings on "the attention theory of value" or "the information economy" describe how, today, simply the activity of watching something on TV or reading something in a magazine or playing something on our computer – i.e. giving something a bit of our attention – creates value for someone, somewhere.[23] And because any form of attention is a freely exerted focusing of our individual perception, memory, language and thinking, the new technologies could be said to capitalise on the very production of subjectivity.

This analysis of production shifts attention away from our roles as meaning-generating users or consumers of TV. Instead the focus turns towards the way in which TV uses us as human machines: we are now seen as intrinsic parts of TV, parts of its input and output, feedback and circuitry. Here, the TV viewer is primarily the synapses or relay through which information is passed on, so that energy can be accumulated and value created.[24] This type of focus notably takes little interest in the communication or interpretation of messages or images: interest is primarily centred on the way in which TV functions as a catalyst for various existential functions. Human consciousness is then understood as one of the elements that belong to the televisual machine itself, and no longer just to an "external" handling of its messages. This perspective perhaps makes it easier to

[22] Lazzarato, op.cit, pp.57.
[23] Beller, Jonathan, "Kino-I, Kino-World: Notes on the Cinematic Mode of Production", i Nicholas Mirzoeff (red.) *The Visual Culture Reader*, Routledge, London 1998, s. 60-86.
[24] Lazzarato, op.cit., pp. 137-138.

see the specific form of control characteristic of today's biopolitical production: whereas the older disciplinary society tended to "mould" or "cast" its subjects within the precise timeframes of closed systems (schools, the military, factories, etc.), the event-like, "cognitive", time-frames of the televisual forms of control are better understood as modulations that will perpetually change from one moment to another.[25] Television is the technological correlate to the continual, "creative" and aesthetically oriented production of our own selves.

V

The contemporary lamp works return to this wider understanding of "televisual production" that informed early video art. But as they do so, they also displace the habitual focus on video art as an "artistic medium" or set of genre conventions and modes of display. The lamp figures emphatically associate "televisual production" with open-ended environmental or atmospheric assemblages, so as to make sure that focus will at least momentarily turn to its production of spaces and social relations, rather than its specific images or messages. But the lamps in question are not just space-creating dispensers of electrical light. The lamps deployed in recent art are also highly visible design objects, present in a great number of shapes and forms that speak loudly of changing fashions, aesthetic sensibilities and social or historical contexts. And this feature is in fact entirely central to their connection with real-time media. Through the lamp figures, televisual production is quite specifically associated with the contemporary cult of everyday creativity. The intensified emphasis on architectural, design and fashion styles that shapes today's environments is actually one of the "productions" of television: it is, quite simply, the spatial practice of the production of subjectivity.

This perspective has consequences for the reading of the preoccupation with architecture, design and fashion that marks recent art. And, as an extension of this, it has consequences for the more general understanding of the life/ art project of the 20th century avant-garde movements. It means having to put to one side the predominant narrative in which the lamp works are inscribed: the story

---

[25] Deleuze, Gilles, "Postscript on the Societies of Control", in *October 59* (Winter 1992), MIT Press, pp. 3-7.

of art rubbing up against the use-oriented practices of design and architecture. The critical framework revolves around a concern with the limits of "pure" vs. "user-oriented" arts or aesthetic practices. The work of lamp creator Jorge Pardo is thus typically said to inhabit "the grey area between art and architecture, art and design and between art and life".[26] But this grey area seems to have a quite precise discursive function: it is described as the place where the limits of the different artistic disciplines are negotiated. Pardo's work is said to be "about the speculation of an object and its definition as art", about using "the language of design to explore and question the conventional limits of sculpture.[27] Pardo is subsequently said to be "an artist who has a command of design and industrial material rather than a designer seeking alternative marketing strategies" – clearly an important clarification since the lamps he creates are both utilitarian and exotically "artistic" in their design. Their problematic utilitarian aspect is described in ingenuously formal terms as an ability to construct axes and points of orientation within the spaces to which he contributes: they "provide light for an entire bar area", and "conceptually lead you from the front of the restaurant to the back rooms".[28]

However, the underlying tenet of this discussion is a legalistic discourse fundamentally concerned with the freedoms or constraints dispensed by various aesthetic practices and their rules. It is a discourse that is heir to almost a century of modernist art balancing between formalist media-specificity and non-formalist interdisciplinary intervention in "the real world" – an eternal dialectics of limits and boundaries that is grounded in the changing viewpoints of a politics of liberation. But what this type of narrative obscures is precisely the way in which the avant-garde art life/ art project and its break with the disciplinary frameworks of "pure" art is implicated in the new forms of production and control. For it is hard not to see this anti-disciplinary and media-oriented art of events, forces, modulations and relationships as an arena for the development, promotion and legitimisation of the key elements at work in the new biopolitical production. Its promotion of concepts like interdisciplinary and process-orientated has no doubt functioned as a real

[26] Mahony, Emma, "The House on the Hill", in CIRCA 97, Autumn 2001, pp. 23-25.
[27] Goldstein, Ann, quoted in Emma Mahony, "The House on the Hill", in CIRCA 97, Autumn 2001, pp. 23-25.
[28] Press release for Jorge Pardo's exhibition at LOT 61, 1997.

point of connection with common culture. At the same time, the avant-garde's life/ art practice could be seen as the locus where the manifestations of this new control culture are made visible as *forms*. Such forms may have all the appeal of models or ideals – models for new ways of fusing work and life, for instance. But they can also take on all the absurdity or strangeness that may come with making visible what is otherwise too self-evident to be remarkable.

A work by another notable lamp-maker and super-stylish "design artist" – Tobias Rehberger – is instructive in this context: it mainly seems to materialise or give form to the life/ time modulation of avant-garde art in its intimate association with mediatic real-time production. It is yet another video work, a wall projection that gives us nothing but pure colour emanations: the changing colours shape the atmosphere of the room the way a mood lamp does. Entitled *81 Years*, the duration of the work is precisely that of a lifetime: the average life expectancy of a person in a Western European country. In the course of those 81 years, the work presents the entire range of colour nuances that video light signals can possibly produce, slowly moving from one end of the spectrum to the other. The computer program that runs the work ensures that something is continually happening (pixel by pixel, from one end of the screen to the other, a change of nuance always takes place) but the change itself is imperceptible to the human eye. Only by leaving the work and coming back weeks later may one – perhaps – note a visible change.

The most immediate impression of the work is then that there is nothing to "see" in it. The work is an event that overturns all expectations about media "visuality", wipes out all traces of TV "content". Here, television appears in its most raw or reduced state: as a pure dispenser of light and time, a real-time machine that is also an existential machine. This is why this dispensing of time cannot be framed, surveyed or controlled by a human consciousness that watches it from the outside, so to speak. No-one will ever be able to "view" the entire work. Its time material may be manipulated in a way that could be understood as a form of time travel: the computer program clock can "fast forward" or "rewind" the signal feed to any desired year (the colours get a bit more interesting after the first couple of decades – in the beginning there are mainly black and greys). What cannot be done, however, is to compress the work into an "accessible" media format. Its time-production can never be encompassed by a more general temporality. The work is thus a form of existence that can only be *encountered* or crossed by other existences. It envelops human perception and memory rather than being enveloped by it. Perception and memory – thinking – works *in* it, not *on* it, and the endless flexibility of the real-time machinery actually makes it possible to imagine all sorts of affective or "thought-like" contractions and distributions of this palette. The work could – in principle – *generate any sort of image*. A veritable toolbox of video or television production, the work then demonstrates that what real-time produces is in fact nothing *but* potential: new time, new moments – the building blocks of the scenario mentality. *81 years* is quite simply a monument to TV as an existential operator. Generating its own "time" and its own form of "thinking" it is, however, not directly harnessed to economic production. As it engages with the qualitative, embodied dimensions of TV time, it opens up a politics of time, perhaps even a momentary liberation of productive time itself.

References

Abrams, M.H. 1971, *The Mirror and the Lamp. Romantic Theory and the Critical Tradition*, Oxford University Press.

Beller, Jonathan 1998, "Kino-I, Kino-World: Notes on the Cinematic Mode of Production", i Nicholas Mirzoeff (red.) *The Visual Culture Reader, Routledge*, London, s. 60-86.

Benjamin, Walter 1963, *Das Kunstwerk im Zeitalter seiner Technischen Reprodusierbarkeit,* Frankfurt/Main: Suhrkamp.

Bergson, Henri 1991, *Matter and Memory*, Translated by N.M. Paul and W.S. Palmer, New York: Zone Book.

Böhme, Gernot 1995, *Atmosphäre. Essays zur neuen Ästhetik*. Suhrkamp Verlag, Frankfurt.

Daniels, Dieter 2002, *Kunst als Sendung, Von der Telegraphie zum Internet*, München: Verlag C.H. Beck.

Deleuze, Gilles, "Postscript on the Societies of Control", in October 59 (Winter 1992), MIT Press, pp. 3-7.

Deleuze, Gilles 1988, *Foucault*. Translated by Sean Hand. University of Minnesota Press.

Deleuze, Gilles and Guattari 1984, Felix, *Anti-Oedipus*, translated by Robert Hurley, Mark Seem and Helen R. Lane, London: Athlone Press.

Dominique Gonzales-Foerster 1999, Pierre Huyghe, Philippe Parreno. Exhibitions catalogue, Musée d'art Moderne de la Ville de Paris.

Foucault, Michel 1979, *The History of Sexuality, Vol. I. An Introduction*. London: Allen Lane.

Foucault, Michel 2003, *Society Must Be Defended. Lectures at the Collège de France 1975-76*, New York: Picador.

Foucault, Michel 1991, "Governmentality", in Graham Burchell, Colin Gordon & Peter Miller, *The Foucault Effect: Studies in Governmentality*, Harvester Wheatsheaf, pp. 87-104.

Hansen, Mark, *New Philosophy for New Media*, MIT Press, 2006

Hardt, Michael and Negri, Antioni 2000, *Empire*, Cambridge University Press.

Lemke, Thomas, "A Zone of Indistinction. A Critique of Giorgio Agambens Concept of Biopolitics", in *Outlines. Critical Social Studies*, Vol. 7, No. 1, 2005, pp. 3-13.

Lazzarato, Maurizio 2002, *Videophilosophie, Zeitwahrnähmung im Postfordismus*, B-Books, Berlin.

Mahony, Emma, "The House on the Hill", in *CIRCA 97*, Autumn 2001, pp. 23-25.

McLuhan, Marshall 1994, *Understanding Media. The Extensions of Man*, The MIT Press.

Weber, Samuel, Mass Mediauras 1996, *Form, Technics, Media*, Stanford University Press.

Synne Skjulstad

Clashing Constructs in Web Design

Introduction

Multiple constructions

Websites pose a number of challenges for description and interpretation. This is largely because the landscapes of web design no longer follow pre-established theoretical maps. Theoretical appoaches to web design and websites are still emerging in a number of domains, not all of which are interrelated or in dialogue with one another. Emerging web texts also pose more specific challenges to established non-digitally mediated aesthetics.

Websites occur in a medley of formats – as slick corporate promotional sites, online bookstores, amateurish personal home pages, as instances of cutting edge visual design and net art. Regardless of the diversity of expression in these environments, as mediating texts they tend to be squeezed into the concepts of 'web pages' or 'websites'. How these websites are understood in terms of communication is, however, surprisingly seldom discussed.

When researching the web, as with any media form, there is potential for confusion, as the medium can be approached from different theoretical and practical positions, or combinations of these.[1] How conceptions of the Web and of websites differ and sometimes clash is striking when websites are approached from a communication design perspective. Seen from such a perspective, one of the main clashes is related to the role of graphic design and usability. Cloninger states:

> There is an unarticulated war currently raging among those who make web sites. Like the war between dark- and light-skinned blacks in Spike

[1] See Wakeford (2000:31), Bolter (2003a), and Bolter (2003b) for discussions of relationships between theory and practice in humanistic studies of new media.

> Lee's *School Daze*, this conflict is one that only its participants recognise. The war is not between commercial sites and experimental sites. It's not between "Bloggers" and "Flashers." This war is between usability experts and graphic designers (Curt Cloninger 2000).

Other clashes relate to contrasting views of websites as either information or mediation. In addition, divergent views on the materiality of web communication in terms of transparency and reflectivity result in contrasting approaches to practice and research in web domains. This essay looks at these clashes between differing conceptions of websites from a communication design perspective. The role of aesthetics is considered important within such a perspective. Aesthetics may be seen as integral to web communication, going beyond the idea that it is merely superficial visual embellishment or a part of a site's usability.

Communication design perspectives

Given these opposing views of the Web, it is important to understand how websites are designed as means of communication. A communication design perspective involves an integrative notion of websites in which the connections and distinctions of aesthetics and functionalities of content, form, system and structure are seen as art and as artful expressions that are woven together in actual web texts[2]. This refers to the level of textual mediation, and not primarily to the study of art at the level of historically situated art objects, experience, or usability.[3] In adapting a communication design approach to websites as mediated texts we may include a variety of interlinked elements as integral to web mediation. These cover graphic design, computer systems design and information architecture. To take such an integrated view contrasts seeing these features

---

[2] Manoff (2006) discusses problems which arise when regarding virtual texts as not connected to the materiality of their mediations. Gitelman (2006:7) argues for regarding media materiality as strongly interconnected with its content. Information, she argues, can therefore not be conceived of as separated from the media that helps define this content. Skjulstad (2007, forthcoming) discusses the mediational aspects of navigation in web designers' portfolios, arguing that design for interaction in websites also can be regarded as important in mediation for communication.

[3] See for example Nielsen (2000) and Norman (1988) for influential inquiries into usability for design and assessment within the technology-centred field of Human-Computer Interaction. See for example Greene (2004), and Paul (2003) for such accounts of electronic art. See McCarthy and Wright (2004) for detailed inquiries into technology as felt and lived experience, Norman (2004) for discussions on emotional design rooted in engineering and cognitive psychology.

in isolation, or accounting for multiple media as communicating individually within the same multimodal text.[4]

A communication-oriented approach is important, because until recently web related research has tended to focus on features other than mediation. Weight has been placed on the role of use and users of the Web.[5] In contrast, researchers have begun to focus on the Web as a rhetorical domain.[6] Studies have been conducted into the aesthetics and style of websites, which are not widely conceived of as art. From a design historical point of view, Engholm (2004) discusses analytic strategies and the categorisation of websites through concepts of technical construction, functionality and aesthetics, but focuses primarily on aesthetics as related to styles and genres in graphic design. Munster (2003), however, regards websites composed in the Software *Macromedia Flash* as affording a flattened and intensified aesthetics. In contrast to many commercial, corporate, and generically designed websites, we find that designers' self-presentations have not received much analytical attention as design for communication.[7] More recently, humanist researchers have also begun to pay attention to experience and performativity relating to digital design.[8] Challenges in theorising and understanding websites in terms of communication design partly lie in the traditional dichotomies of form and function, and written text and image. Most of all, these challenges are rooted in the various histories and accounts of the Web as a structure, a communication medium and a network for social interaction, resulting in differing notions of what web design is and how it might better be understood.

So as to further develop a communication design oriented perspective on web design, it is therefore fruitful to take a closer look at the colliding conceptions outlined above. I will do this by first examining two main aspects of web design as fields of design practice – web

---

[4] Kress and van Leeuwen (2001) present a theory of multimodal discourse where communication resources, what they refer to as *modes*, are seen as to be communicating different things within complex texts.

[5] Turkle (1995) inquires into issues of identity in online domains in her book *Lives on the Screen.*

[6] Fagerjord (2003) applies the term rhetorical convergence in his accounts of multimediational rhetorics in web mediation, whereas Liestøl (1999) applies rhetorics as a theoretical framework in his essays on hypermedia design.

[7] Web designers' online portfolios and project presentations as mediations are discussed in terms of communication design by Skjulstad (2007, forthcoming).

[8] Tronstad (2004) applies the concept of performativity to account for users' activities in texts based computer games.

design as information and the web as a visual domain – along with their related research discourses where these clashes are most striking.

Outline

In the first section, I outline how our understanding of web design has been conceived in terms of information and related notions of usability, and their force in framing much of the analysis of web-mediated communication. After this, I discuss the role and influence of artistic and aesthetic approaches to web design. This is followed by discussing the web as a visual design domain that takes up the role communication design might have in umpiring between usability driven approaches and visual aesthetic ones. I close with concluding remarks about implications of a communication design perspective that transverses these positions and that acknowledge the importance of aesthetic studies of the web.

Web design as information

Immaterial information

Tim Berners-Lees' initial conception of the Web, as "... a distributed collaborative multimedia information system" [9] was closely connected to ideas about making information immaterial, as well as collective reading and writing practices already existing within research communities preoccupied with hypertext.[10] The early days of the Web were dominated by education and research institutions,[11] and at the time there already existed several hypermedia systems which were thoroughly researched and developed through practice-based research.[12] Hypertext drew humanist researchers to the study of non-linear digital

---

[9] Paul (2003:111).

[10] Ted Nelson coined the term hypertext in the 1960s. He defined hypertext like this; "... Let me introduce the word "hypertext" to mean a body of written or pictorial material interconnected in such a complex way that it could not conveniently be presented on paper" (Nelson 1965:96).

[11] Paul (2003:8).

[12] Two hypertext systems developed before the Web were *Intermedia* and *Storyspace*. *Intermedia* was developed at Brown University, and *Storyspace* was developed at Eastgate systems during the 1980s. Both systems were researched and developed through practice-based research, as discussed by Bolter (2003), and more extensively in terms of hypertext by Landow (1997).

text and the Web. As part of the growth of the Internet,[13] from its inception the Web was about popular use and moves from university domains to public access. It did not, however, afford collaborative writing as well as earlier stand-alone hypertext tools. In its infancy, the Web was partly seen as an inferior system in comparison to those used to produce fiction and non-fiction.[14] Just as Berners-Lee initially saw the Web as a space "in which information could exist",[15] it was not primarily developed as a medium for visual communication. This initial view of the Web as dealing with immaterial digital information was later to be taken up by the usability community. Such a conception clashes significantly with those stemming from practitioners from the field of graphic design, who in time entered the domain of web design.

A new tag in town

As a distributed network medium, the Web popularised ideas developed and investigated within earlier hypertext research communities. Tim Berners-Lee was a visionary computer engineer, and not a visual artist or visual specialist. The Web that he founded was launched as a Universal application for connecting documents across computers, and for interlinking between documents and passages of written text. HTML (Hypertext Markup Language) was the computer language developed by Berners-Lee for representing web pages as hypertext.

The term web pages has been widely used to refer to what are more accurately labelled websites. In these sites, HTML was gradually extended to allow for the publication of more than alphanumeric text. New tags in HTML, along with developments in browsers, eventually allowed the insertion of images into websites, thereby opening up the textual environment for decorative and aesthetic choices, and in particular for visual communication beyond the written word. This was important in contributing to a gradual development of the Web as a visual medium.

The users' choice

Drawing on an established tradition of Human-Computer Interaction (HCI), early views of web design resonated with those

---

13 Berners-Lee (2000:7).

14 See Landow (1997) for a discussion of the differences between the Web and other hypertext systems, and Berners-Lee (2000) for accounts of how the hypertext research communities were not initially overly interested in the Web.

15 Berners-Lee (2000:39).

of hypertext researchers and their focus on users' power to manipulate and change online texts according to their needs. In this view, graphic representation should not be directly tied to the information on the Web, and the 'content' of web pages was to be subjected to the users' choices of presentation. From a computer scientists' or engineers' view, this potential for customisation of screen layout was seen as one of the great features of the Web. Such functionality suited the needs of visually impaired people, and also provided a visual and presentational flexibility not found in written publications. This view rests on an understanding of websites as entities containing autonomous information, which can be separated from their mediated form without significant changes in mediated meaning. Manoff (2006), however, criticises notions of immateriality of electronic texts. She argues for the importance of seeing digital texts as embodying distinct materialities depending on the platform, interface, standards and coding used. She argues that this helps the digital humanities avoid prevailing notions that rest on the assumption that "... the text or content can exist in some pure platonic form ready to be poured into whatever format or container is most convenient".[16]

In the early 1990s, when the Web was still a very young medium, mediational conventions were formed through experimental presentational practice. Some developers and designers rejected the importance of the presentation of information completely, and even saw it as undermining the Web as an immaterial information space. Much creativity and effort was spent on trying to teach inexperienced web users how to navigate these new information spaces, so as to avoid becoming 'lost in cyberspace'. Web-based interaction design as a field was still largely to be developed, and professionals and non-professionals alike tried to create websites that were easy for users to access and experience. As the new medium became subject to extensive visual, structural and technological experimentation, the figure who later became the main spokesperson for web usability, Jacob Nielsen, entered the stage.

Usability

Nielsen aimed to help developers and enterprises avoid some of the worst 'mistakes' in web design. One of these mistakes was perceived as being giving attention to aesthetics. Nielsen developed a normative

16 Manoff (2006:315).

approach referred to as 'Usability'. His approach was to focus on the users of online web texts, and to help designers facilitate users' efforts at traversing the new medium. The main idea behind usability is that the Web is an information space, where the user is a goal-oriented information seeker, and the web designer's role is to help her or him to achieve their informational goals. According to Nielsen, this is to perform useful tasks. Nielsen has argued that "There are essentially two basic approaches to web design: the artistic ideal of expressing yourself and the engineering ideal of solving a problem for a customer."[17] Nielsen regarded communication design and aesthetic or artistic practice as subordinate to commercial activity. He asserted that: "While I acknowledge that there is a need for art, fun, and a general good time on the Web, I believe that the main goal of most web projects should be to make it easy for customers to perform useful tasks".[18]

However, we may ask just what is a useful task? Nielsen operates in a tradition where the web interface is not supposed to draw attention to itself, but rather work as a clear and uncluttered channel for effective communication. Within this view, graphics are regarded as only slowing down the loading of each page, and aesthetics is considered as causing confusion and delays.

However, not all web users are doing the same things when accessing, traversing and delving into the Web. A 'task', as referred to by Nielsen, might be to purchase an item, or find an address or develop an overview of certain domains. Importantly, it might also be to find and view interesting and puzzling designs, have a look at the experimental or creative web design scene, and use sites for purposes that exceed the orientation towards performance of easily definable tasks. Within this approach, open-ended and explorative web use tends to be regarded as less important and less specific, and is therefore not discussed much at all.

Such a functionalist approach to web design sets up an unproductive and binary distinction between usefulness and aesthetics. User friendliness is applauded because it helps users do what they are trying to do on the Web. Aesthetics is considered ineffective and redundant because elaborate and creative experiments in web design are blamed for obscuring the delivery of information. Purposively, information rules. Designers who grapple with new ways of designing inventive

---

17 Nielsen (2000:11).
18 Nielsen (2000:11).

and visually rich websites are seen as alienating users. However, this has not been a blanket approach of HCI researchers.

Aesthetics in HCI

The field of HCI is one of the domains of research and development ascribed the role as main supplier of concepts, theories and methods of inquiry into digital interfaces.[19] Questions about relations between HCI and aesthetics have been taken up more recently after a growing focus on topics beyond effectiveness and task orientation. For researchers such as Hassenzahl, aesthetics is regarded as a measurable quality inherent to some degree in digital objects, such as the skin of a media player or the interfaces of ATMs.[20] This renewed interest in aesthetics in HCI is often referred to as "the aesthetic turn", aiming at extending the field to include more than a strict focus on functionality.[21]

One important feature of many contemporary websites is that functionality tends to be deeply integrated into the visual character of the sites. In computer system-centric approaches to web design, aesthetic features tend to be conceived of as embellishing graphic elements in the 'presentational layer' on top of the system in a digital artefact. This situates aesthetics as superficial styling, with little reference to the overall communicational potential of the artefacts. In guides to the development of digital artefacts this layer tends to be described as the last step in the design process. This 'presentational' layer[22] is another term for the icing on the cake, which is considered important, but not essential. The peer-reviewed academic journal "Human Computer Interaction" ran a special issue on the role of beauty in HCI in 2004. The leading article by Hassenzahl investigated the relationship between usability and beauty in a positivist experiment. Participants rated the degree of beauty of different surfaces, 'skins', or in other words, the icing, of a digital music player. Data were used to see if beauty could influence perceived usability because of aesthetics. This illustrates rather well the prevailing notions of aesthetics within one of the main publishers. In short, the relevance of aesthetics in digital artefacts is dependent on whether or not it enhances usability.

19 Udsen and Jørgensen (2005:205).
20 See Hassenzahl (2004).
21 Udsen and Jørgensen (2005:206).
22 See Garrett (2003) for accounts of interaction design which divides digital design processes into "layers" or "spheres", thereby separating practices and design levels from each other.

Usability is important in thoughtfully[23] designing artefacts that are easy to use, but is not a sufficiently flexible concept to embody user friendliness outside the scope of task-orientation.

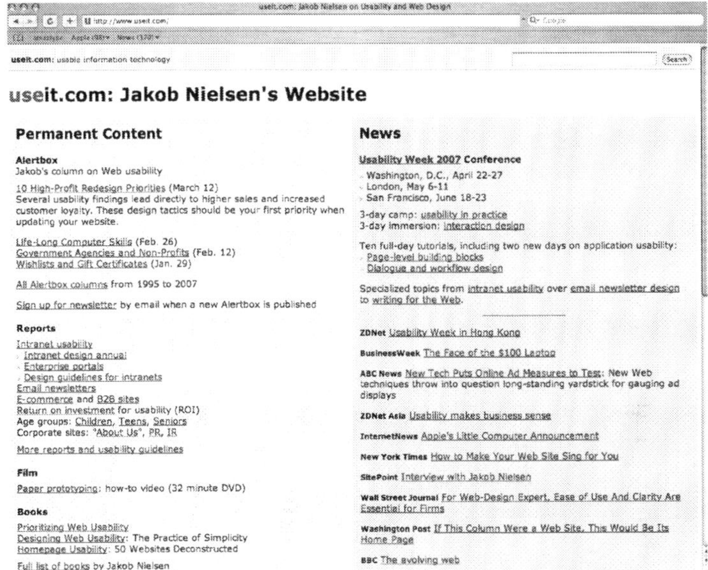

Figure 1. Screen grab from www.useit.com, exemplifying how the leading usability expert Jacob Nielsen conceptualize a user-friendly web site. All the links appear as blue underlined words. The colors are kept in blue and yellow as this is considered the most readable color combinations.

Usability 'rules'

Many of the guidelines proposed by Nielsen have now become conventions in web design. Nielsen lists the main rules for good usability. When followed, these rules help web developers to create websites that are easy to use and which allow universal access. This approach importantly includes sight-impaired users and users with slow connections.[24] On the other hand a mediational conservatism is inherent in the usability perspective, as it does not welcome experimentation or emergent designs. Usability therefore leaves limited room for artistic practice or for developmental design processes that work across different media types.

---

[23] See Löwgren and Stolterman (2004) on thoughtful interaction design.

[24] See Nielsen (2000).

Usability rules may be utterly broken – and with interesting results, as net artists *jodi.org* demonstrated in the late 1990s. The designers of this site developed a meta-site about web design, which violated many of the rules set up by usability theorists and practitioners. These net artists demonstrated that web design could also be something more than a means of enacting effective e-commerce and solving strictly defined problems. Web design could also be art. The insistence of net artists on bending and transgressing the functionalism of usability approaches would raise a new set of communicative issues for web design.

The Web as a visual design domain

Window and mirror

What happened, then, as the Web gradually morphed into a colourful and visual medium? Bolter and Gromala discuss conflicts which arose between usability experts and graphic designers. They divide the opposing positions into two broad groups, which they refer to as 'the structuralists' and 'the designers.'[25]

> We are talking about two competing visions of digital technology: the pragmatic vision offered by Norman and other HCI experts, for whom computers are information appliances, and the vision offered by digital artists and interaction designers. They are competing in the sense that each vision is an attempt to convince our culture at large (Bolter and Gromala 2003:3).

These conflicting views are deeply rooted in the genesis and history of the Web as a multi-medium which initially was driven by development of technology. These polarised positions, rooted in computer science on one hand, and in the shift from "page to screen"[26] for graphic design on the other, present challenges for our understanding of websites at a textual level, and when approaching web design in terms of communication and not primarily in terms of usability.

A metaphorical approach to web design

Few efforts have been made to provide a coherent and extensive history of the graphic and aesthetic aspects of web design.[27]

---

[25] See Bolter and Gromala (2003:3).

[26] Snyder (1998) looks at changing literacies fuelled by changing information and communication technologies, going from "page" to "screen".

[27] Engholm (2002:193).

Developments in graphic design for the Web were closely tied to developments in web browsers and HTML code. The Web can be said to have taken a more visual turn as the possibilities for inclusion of images and graphics were extended. Even as early as 1993, the mark-up was expanded making it possible to create not only web pages with images but also moving image in the form of GIF animations.[28] From being predominantly an environment of written information, the Web started to fill up with colour, images and animations. This graphic expansion of the designers' visual repertoire was a joy to some, and a source of frustration for others.[29]

David Siegel, a graphic designer, entered web design from the domain of graphic design for print media, as did many other professionals.[30] He has been considered a pioneer in developing graphic elements in web design through the emphasis he has placed on the ability of graphic designers to create visual experiences, as opposed to information displays and structures.[31] In 1997, he proposed ways to create 'killer websites' through graphic design. His position was a direct counterpoint to a usability-dominated approach. However, to allow graphic designers more freedom to shape websites as they wanted, HTML needed to offer a richer set of possibilities.[32] This need led many graphic designers into hard-nosed programming and computing in order to improve the somewhat limited and immature tools they had at hand. Computer engineers and graphic designers now found they had web design in common, but had quite divergent conceptions of their shared medium.

Siegel claimed that the best experience could be provided by graphic designers, who through their visual competence knew how to present and organise information better than average users or programmers could. So Siegel, perhaps unknowingly, became a spokesperson for a view of web design that was followed by several designers who experimented their way through this new medium. Siegel saw the Web as

---

[28] See Engholm (2002) for a historical account for this expansion.

[29] Munster (2003:135).

[30] Siegel launched the influential guide to visually oriented web design *Creating Killer Websites* in 1997.

[31] Engholm discusses this in detail (2002:194).

[32] Siegel (1997:4) gives a personal account of his experiences with HTML, making analogies between letting users decide the graphic design in websites and telling a painter how to hold the brushes.

more than a place for unhindered creativity; it was also a place where graphic design enhanced market oriented communication.[33]

Many graphic designers took an active part in shaping the Web even further in the direction of a multimodal environment. This process changed many graphic designers' professional identities as many of them increasingly became web developers, working deep down in changing the codes that made up the medium to which they had turned their attention.[34] Others geared their creativity away from strictly commercial web communication and developed many of the now canonical net art sites. These sites offer an alternative view of the Web to that of a neutral informational medium, and are inscribed into works of art that experimented with representations and mediations of time, space and movement. This move towards artistic creativity and innovation in form and function polarised views on web design further. What was important, however, in the artistic compositions on the Web, was a focus on expressivity and visual communication that could not be mapped or adequately framed in a functionalist approach to usability.

Net art: the Web as a medium for artistic practice

The Web is now an established domain for artistic practice and net art is now a field in its own right. Works of net art have in common that they apply the Internet, and in many cases the Web, for artistic purposes both as a medium of production, and as a medium for distribution.[35] What characterises much artistic practice on the Web is the ability and will to push or bend established practices of web communication beyond common use. Works of net art may serve as examples of conceptions of web design which have taken yet another step away from an approach to the Web as a domain for the performance of "useful tasks". Rachel Green describes net art as follows:

> Though their tools and venues differ, Internet art is underwritten by the motivations that have propelled nearly all artistic practices: ideology; technology; desire; the urge to experiment, communicate, critique or

---

[33] Rivett (2000) points out that even if Siegel is credited with introducing a greater focus on visual design on the Web, he still operates within a domain of commercial persuasive discourse.

[34] See Stocker and Schöpf (2001) for a discussion of digital art as a multiply layered domain of digital professional practices where the participants do not primarily regard themselves as artists.

[35] See Paul (2003:8).

> destroy; the elaboration of ideals or emotions; and memorialising observation or experience (Greene 2004:12).

Early net art such as *jodi.org* draws attention to the medium, and may therefore be described in terms of hypermediacy,[36] or reflectivity.[37] Hypermediacy refers to media expressions that draw attention to themselves as mediated. In their site *Jodi.org* from 1995, they created "... aggressively technical interfaces, ignoring coherent content in favour of desultory representations of code, protocols and operating system aesthetics inside out".[38] Such aestheticisation of the computer system is evident in the web-based artwork of *jodi.org*. The images in Figure 2 show visual representations of computer code as presented through the browser. When the HTML code of this site was viewed as *code*, however, it appeared as figurative patterns of technical diagrams. *Jodi.org* is an early example of non-usability, and demonstrates that mediation is taking place in the interfaces between surface and the system of websites. *Jodi.org* is clearly designed as a meta-comment on the entire web medium.

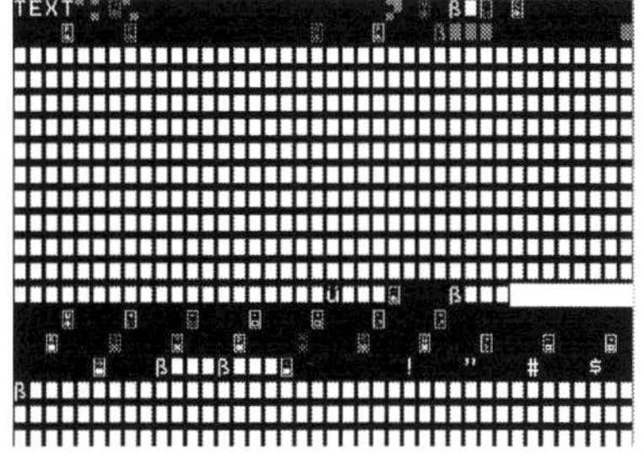

Figure 2. Screen grabs showing the web design from jodi.org.

Whilst in the Renaissance Alberti tried to make the canvas become invisible by creating an illusion of a window into a virtual painted world, net art often does the opposite by letting the medium be the message, in McLuhan's words.[39] As opposed to a neutral information space, web interfaces were not only conceptualised as transparent, but also as reflective projections of the Web medium itself. We might say, then, that subsequent to the emergence of net art and a visual,

---

[36] Bolter and Grusin (1999:31).
[37] Bolter and Gromala (2003:62).
[38] Greene (2004:40).
[39] See McLuhan (1964:7).

graphical turn in web design the 'the lines were drawn' between usability and visualisation.

Umpiring between the sides: communication design

Aesthetic practice

Like other kinds of visual design, web design has now matured into a visual domain in its own right, and with related rich and complex means of expression.[40] Yet, there has been little focus placed on websites as an expressive media form, and the literature available on web related topics is dominated by 'how-to-do-it' books and manuals. More academically, Cloninger (2002) introduces style as a concept for categorisation of websites, but does not account for the roots of these styles in the history of graphic design.[41] Graphic design and concepts of style tend to be seen either as isolated features of websites or as superficial embellishment. Aesthetics in web design thus remains under-articulated.

Web design has been analysed in terms of a history of styling, but different styles of functionality and interaction are barely mentioned.[42] The focus of researchers striving to escape the dominant functionalist approaches to web design, and rather engage with aesthetics and expressivity, tends not to account very well for how the computer system and organisation of a site may also be the outcome of aesthetic practice. In investigations of web texts, few analytical approaches to the role of aesthetics in digital artefacts take into account the computer system, such as a navigational system, organization of categories, menus, and the site's overall interaction design. Consequently, such investigations fail to address important features of web design, for example the interaction design and architecture of a web site.[43]

In general, discussions of the relevance of aesthetics in web design within humanist approaches are sparse. Works that are discussed in terms of electronic art are often accounted for in terms of their role in the history of electronic art. Websites, however, may be blends of genres and may well be an advert, an art project and a research and

---

[40] Engholm (2002:193).

[41] Engholm (2002:195).

[42] Engholm points to the lack of analytical attention to websites (2002:193).

[43] Questions as to what may be regarded as media in web-based communication are discussed by Skjulstad (2007, forthcoming). Mediatized navigation through *Flash* animation exemplifies that design for interaction is an integral part of web mediation.

development project all in one.[44] Therefore, many web mediations fall into an analytic void. The existing analytical discourses tend to approach aesthetics either as a troubling, or important but unclear factor, or reduce notions of aesthetics to categories of visual styles in web design.

Several web texts, such as for example the web project *amaztype*, shown in Figure 3, demonstrate that it is not possible to locate aesthetic practice in web design in a constructed notion of a top layer, a skin, or some specific feature of a design as suggested by Hassenzahl (2004). There is more to this website than the immediate graphic design that is visible in the web interface that makes up this site.

The importance of a perspective on web design that takes both interface and system into account may be illustrated by this website. Designed by Keita Kitamura and Yugo Nakamura, *Amaztype* immediately draws us into some of the core problems facing humanistic oriented inquiry into mediation, aesthetics and usability in websites. By focusing only on visual design in the traditional sense, one may overlook the fact that this site is a drastically rearranged version of the online bookstore *amazon.com*, turned into a typeface. Instead of seeing visual interface design and computer systems design separately, in this instance it is fruitful to regard them as part of the overall communication design in which the computer system and aesthetics are deeply intertwined.

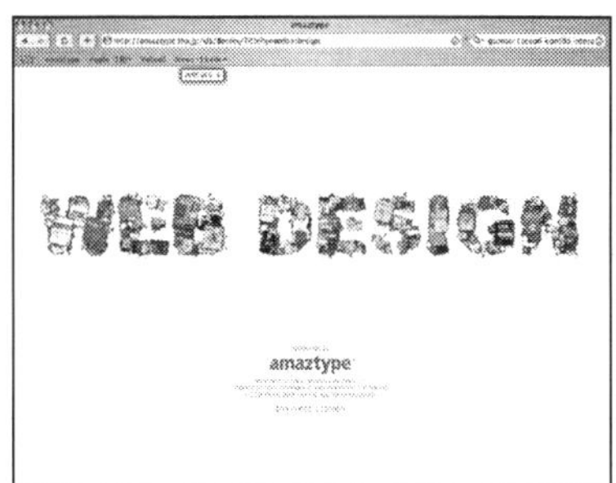

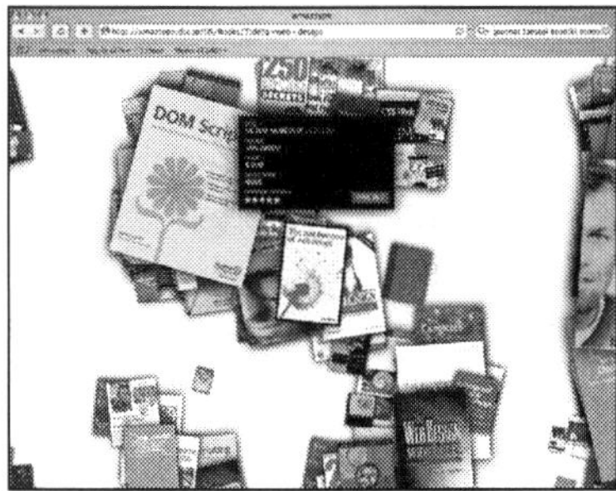

Figure 3. Screen grabs showing the web application "Amaztype". The application is simultaneously a typeface and a visualised search engine for the collection of books stored in the database of the online bookstore "amazon.com".

This website serves as an alternative interface to the online bookstore *amazon.com.* Amaztype is connected to the database of this store and applies the same data as the store. The "content" in this

[44] Gibbons (2005) takes up related blends of professions, practices and genres in her book on the relationship between art and advertising.

application may therefore be described as the same as in the bookstore. The organisation and presentation of these data, however, is altered almost beyond recognition in *amaztype*. As well as being an alternative interface to the online bookstore, *amaztype* is a typeface where any word typed into the text field appears on the screen as composed of different book covers available in *amazon.com*. By clicking on the letters in the words, an enlarged view of the chosen letter and the book covers is made available. Windows with information about the selected books may be retrieved as may direct links to all the books in *amazon.com*.

In *amaztype* the underlying computer system has been aestheticisied[45] and conceived of in terms of the reflectivity Bolter and Gromala (2003) have ascribed to the interfaces of digital artefacts. *Amaztype*, however, provides users with other experiences than those offered at *amazon.com*. *Amaztype* affords a visual overview of the number of books available on a topic, and displays the visual representations of actual book covers in virtual piles, much as in an untidy book store. It also demonstrates that the same data can be represented entirely differently in two different websites. Hence, the form and content in such an interface cannot be seen separately.[46]

Aesthetic qualities in *amaztype* may be fruitfully discussed when combining and extending our notions of visual design and usability on the Web to include use beyond that which is geared towards executing specific tasks, such as buying books and writing words on a computer.

Experience design

An alternative strategy for inquiry into the intersections of computing, electronic art, web design and aesthetics is what is now often referred to as experience design. A usability-oriented approach to design for experience is proposed by Norman. He has departed from his initial strict focus on usability,[47] and launched the term 'emotional design'.[48] He approaches emotional design from a cognitive

[45] Welsch (1997) discusses aestheticization processes in relation to popular culture, which extends into advertising and the Internet.

[46] Both Manovich (2001:67) and Manoff (2006) discuss this interrelationship between media content, form and materiality.

[47] In his book *The Design of Everyday Things* (1989) Norman advocates a general usability perspective on design, drawing on examples of everyday objects.

[48] See Norman (2004) on emotional design as an expansion of a strict usability perspective on design.

psychology perspective, and makes a Kantian move in placing beauty not only in the eyes of the beholder, but deep into the core of the human nervous system. Within HCI, an increased focus on experience may solve many problems connected to questions relating to aesthetics and the design of digital artefacts by conveniently removing problems of accounting for aesthetics in digital artefacts. Instead, the focus is on the subjective experiences of users. McCarthy and Wright approach experience with technology as embedded in our everyday lives "… that is open to the sensual, emotional, volitional, and dialogically imaginative aspects of felt experience" (2004:184). They regard the felt and lived experience of technology as going beyond usability or aesthetics.

Embodied interaction may seem to be in contrast with earlier notions of users as immaterial beings in virtual space. The concept of embodied interaction has been taken up recently as an approach to experience, interaction and computing. The focus has been on users' experiences in acting with technologies and relations to bodily experience. This revitalised focus on users' individual or cognitive and phenomenological experiences of using digital artefacts has led researchers within HCI, such as Mazé and Redström, to stress that there has been an overly strong turn away from the computational object, that is digitally designed artefacts, in favour of studies of design processes and use, users' needs, and users' experiences. Mazé and Redström therefore propose we return to the computational object because 'Just as we need methods for exploring use and users, we need methods and frameworks for exploring the designed object'.[49] Such a renewed focus is also a return to placing greater attention on digital texts, such as websites. In my view, however, we also need to see this textual level of analysis as part of a wider contextualised and situated view encompassed by Communication Design.

Textual analysis as a vehicle for addressing mediation in websites may cut across divergent conceptions of web design, as well as making these clashes visible in exploring websites as texts, that is as mediation and communication. Such a focus allows inquiry into and across aesthetics, usability, graphic design, as well as interaction design in websites – without narrowing the focus on these features seen in isolation in analysis of actual sites. Hopefully, such a mode of inquiry allows us

---

[49] Mazé and Redström (2005:8).

to interrelate aspects from usability and visualisation rather than to perpetrate their polarisation at the cost of richer multimodal analysis.

Mediated Aesthetics at Work?

The importance of 'materiality'

In discussing remediation, that is how media refashion themselves in relation to older media forms, Bolter and Grusin point to the enormous diversity in web expression: "Everything, from the snow fields of Antarctica to the deserts of Mars, finds its way on to the web".[50] As we have seen, this diversity brings challenges for practitioners and theorists alike.

A usability-oriented perspective, which regards the Web as a medium for exchange of information, is closely tied to the way the Web was conceived by its initial developers. However, within this conception of the Web as an information space, there is a distinction between the views of some major figures. While Berners-Lee envisioned and developed the web as a universal information space, Nielsen operates at a normative level in relation to actual websites. While Berners-Lee aimed at facilitating distribution of networked information, Nielsen aimed at facilitating business on the Web.

From a humanities perspective, Bolter and Gromala (2003) regard Nielsens' approach as a structuralist conceptualisation of web mediation. In contrast, they cast interfaces in terms of transparency and reflectivity, that is, as mediation. Bolter and Grusin (1999) discuss repurposing of old media forms as remediation. Here they look back to Alberti, and the central perspective as a visual strategy for erasing the focus on the medium, creating an illusion of some kind of reality. In discussions of remediation, they refer to this as immediacy.[51]

Aesthetics and communication design

For media and communication studies – itself moving into 'digital' domains, approaches to analysing web design may fruitfully be regarded through the lens of communication design. Web mediation, in this view, may be seen as embodying several mediational strata. Broadly, communication design is a perspective that takes into account

[50] Bolter & Grusin (1999:210).
[51] Bolter and Grusin (1999:30).

communicative resources in a text, the origins and composition of these resources, and their uses in context, and how these together are realised as communication. A communication design perspective on web design considers websites' functionality, interaction design, architecture, graphic design, media types such as written texts, images, videos and so on as equally important aspects of mediation for communication. At a fundamental level, websites are designed to be communicative. To some extent, designers may need to make normative decisions on the part of users, yet they also need to make room for creative communication and aesthetics at work.

Such a holistic perspective draws on Löwgren and Stolterman's[52] concept of a 'dynamic gestalt'. When this concept is applied to websites, they may be conceived of as more than the sum of their parts. Such an approach makes it possible to experience and to analyse websites in use over time. The value of a communication design perspective is that it allows us to relate surface and system, usability and aesthetics. Communication design might also help us to see past some of the earlier clashing views on the Web.

Acknowledgments

This text is part of an article-based PhD in Media and Communication Studies at InterMedia, University of Oslo. For editing, discussions and constructive suggestions, my thanks to Andrew Morrison at InterMedia, and to all the participants in the *Aesthetics at Work* project.

References

Berners-Lee, Tim 2000, *Weaving the Web: The Past, Present and Future of the World Wide Web*, Texere: London.

Bolter, David Jay & Gromala, Diane 2003, *Windows and Mirrors: Interaction Design, Digital Art, and the Myth of Transparency*, The MIT Press: Cambridge.

Bolter, Jay David & Grusin, Richard 1999, *Remediation; Understanding New Media*, The MIT Press: Cambridge.

52 Löwgren and Stolterman (2004:137).

Bolter, Jay David 2003a, *Critical Theory and the Challenge of New Media,* In Hocks, Mary & Kendrick, Michelle (eds.), *Eloquent Images*, The MIT Press: Cambridge: pp. 19-36.

Bolter, David Jay 2003b, *Theory and Practice in New Media Studies,* In Liestøl, Gunnar, Morrison, Andrew & Rasmussen, Terje (eds.), *Digital Media Revisited: Theoretical and Conceptual Reflections in Digital Domains,* The MIT Press: Cambridge. pp. 13-35.

Bush, Vannevar 1945, "As We May Think", *The Atlantic Monthly*, Vol. 176, No. 1, pp. 101-108.

Cloninger, Curt 2002, *Fresh Styles for Web Designers: Eye Candy from the Underground,* New Riders Publishing: Indianapolis.

Cloninger, Curt 2000, " Usability Experts are from Mars, Graphic designers are from Venus", At http://www.alistapart.com/articles/marsvenus/.

Dourish, Paul 2004, *Where the Action Is: The Foundations of Embodied Interaction,* The MIT Press: Cambridge.

Engholm, Ida 2004, *Webgenrer og Stilarter: Om at Analysere og Kategorisere Websites (Web Genres and Styles: On Analyzing and Categorizing Websites),* In Engholm, Ida & Klastrup, Lisbeth (eds.), *Digitale Verdener (Digital Worlds)*, Gyldendal: Copenhagen, pp. 57-77.

Engholm, Ida 2002, 'Digital Style History: the Development of Graphic Design on the Internet', *Digital Creativity,* Vol. 13, No 4. pp. 193-211.

Engholm, Ida & Salamon, Karen Lisa 2005, 'Web Genres and Styles as Socio-Cultural Indicators – an Experimental, Interdisciplinary Dialogue', *In-the-Making*, 1st *Nordic Design Research Conference*, Copenhagen. 29 – 31 May, At: http://www.tii.se/reform/inthemaking/files/p119.pdf.

Fagerjord, Anders 2003, *Rhetorical Convergence: Studying Web Media*, In Liestøl, Gunnar Morrison, Andrew & Rasmussen, Terje (eds.), *Digital Media Revisited: Theoretical and Conceptual Innovation in Digital Domains*, The MIT Press: Cambridge, p. 225–293.

Friedberg, Anne 2006, *The Virtual Window: From Alberti to Microsoft,* The MIT Press: Cambridge.

Garrett, Jesse James 2003, *The Elements of User Experience: User-Centered Design for the Web*, New Riders Publishing: New York.

Gauntlett, David 2000, "Web Studies: A User's Guide", In Gauntlett, David (ed.), *Web Studies: Rewiring Media Studies for the Digital Age,* Arnold: New York, pp. 2-18.

Gibbons, Joan 2005, *Art and Advertising*, I. B. Tauris: London.

Gitelman, Lisa 2006, *Always Already New: Media, History, and the Data of Culture*, The MIT Press: Cambridge.

Greene, Rachel 2004, *Internet Art,* Thames & Hudson: New York.

Hassenzahl, Marc 2004, "The Interplay of Beauty, Goodness, and Usability in Interactive Products", *Human-Computer Interaction,* Vol. 19, No 4, pp. 319–349.

Jensen, Jens F 1998, *Multimedier, Hypermedier, Interaktive Medier (Multimedia, Hypermedia, Interactive Media),* Aalborg Universitetsforlag: Aalborg.

Kress, Gunther & van Leeuwen, Theo 2001, *Multimodal Discourse: The Modes and Media of Contemporary Communication*, Arnold: London.

Landow, George 1997, *Hypertext 2.0,* The Johns Hopkins Press: Baltimore.

Liestøl, Gunnar 1999, *Essays in Rhetorics of Hypermedia Design*, Unpublished doctoral thesis, University of Oslo: Oslo.

Löwgren, Jonas & Stolterman, Erik 2004, *Thoughtful Interaction Design: a Design Perspective on Information Technology,* The MIT Press: Cambridge.

Manoff, Marlene 2006, "The Materiality of Digital Collections: Theoretical and Historical Perspectives", In *Portal: Libraries and the Academy,* Vol. 6, No. 3, p. 311-325.

Manovich, Lev 2001, *The Language of New Media.* The MIT Press, Cambridge, MA.

Mazé, Ramia & Redström, Johan 2005, "Form and the Computational Object", *Digital Creativity,* Vol. 16, No. 1, p. 7–18.

McCarthy, John & Wright, Peter 2004, *Technology as Experience*, The MIT Press: Cambridge.

McLuhan, Marshall 1964, *Understanding Media: The extension of man*, The MIT Press: Cambridge.

Morrison, Andrew (ed.) 2007, forthcoming, *Inside Multimodal Composition,* Hampton Press, Cresskill.

Munster, Anna 2006, *Materializing New Media: Embodiment in Information Aesthetics,* Dartmouth College Press: Hanover.

Munster, Anna 2003, "Compression and the Intensification of Visual Information in Flash Aesthetics". In *Proceedings of DAC 2003 Conference,* At: http://hypertext.rmit.edu.au/dac/papers/, pp. 135–142.

Murray, Janet 1997, *Hamlet on the Holodeck,* The MIT Press: Cambridge.

Naughton, John 1999, *A Brief History of the Future: The Origins of the Internet,* Weidenfeld & Nicholson: Phoenix.

Nelson, Ted 1965, "A File Structure for the Complex, the Changing and the Indeterminate", In *ACM Proceedings of the 20th National Conference*, New York. p. 84-100.

Nielsen, Jacob 2000, *Designing Web Usability*, New Riders Publishing: Indianapolis.

Norman, A, Donald 1988, *The Design of Everyday Things,* Basic Books: New York.

Norman, Donald 2004, *Emotional Design: Why we Love (or hate) Everyday Things,* Basic Books: New York.

Paul, Christiane 2003, *Digital Art,* Thames & Hudson: London.

Rivett, Miriam 2000, "Approaches to Analyzing the Web Text: A Consideration of the Web Site as an Emergent Cultural Form", In *Convergence,* Vol. 6, No 3, pp. 111-113.

Siegel, David 1996, *Creating Killer Web Sites: The Art of Third-Generation Site Design,* Prentice Hall: Indianapolis.

Skjulstad, Synne 2004, "Flashback: Tracing developments from electronic paper to dynamic digital environments in the software Macromedia Flash", In *Proceedings of the Future Ground Conference 2004*, 17-21 November 2004, Melbourne, Australia, (CD-ROM)

Skjulstad, Synne 2007, forthcoming, "What are These? Designers' Websites as Communication Design", In Morrison, Andrew (ed.), *Inside Multimodal Composition,* Hampton Press: Cresskill.

Snyder, Ilana 1998, *Page to Screen: Taking Literacy into the Electronic Era,* Routledge: London.

Stocker, Gerfried & Schöpf, Christine (eds.) 2001, *Takeover – Who's doing the Art of Tomorrow?,* Springer, Vienna.

Tractinsky, Noam 2004, "A Few Notes on the Study of Beauty in HCI", *Human Computer Interaction*, Vol. 19, No. 4, pp. 351-357.

Tractinsky, Noam 1997, "Aesthetics and Apparent Usability: Empirically Assessing Cultural and Methodological Issues", In *Proceedings of CHI'97*, 22-27 March 1997, Atlanta, Georgia, pp. 115-122.

Tronstad, Ragnhild 2004, *Interpretation, Performance, Play, & Seduction: Textual Adventures in Tubmud*, Unpublished Doctoral Thesis, University of Oslo: Oslo.

Turkle, Sherry 1995, *Life on the Screen: Identity in the Age of the Internet*, Simon & Schuster: New York.

Udsen, Lars Erik & Jørgensen, Helms Anker 2005, "The Aesthetic Turn: Unravelling Recent Aesthetic Approaches to Human-Computer Interaction", *Digital Creativity*, Vol. 16, No. 4, pp. 205-216.

Vartanian, Ivan 2001, *Now Loading: The Aesthetics of Web Graphics*, Gingko Press: Corte Madera.

Wakeford, Nina 2000, New Media, New Methodologies: Studying the Web, In Gauntlett, David (ed), *Web Studies: Rewiring Media Studies for the Digital Age,* Arnold: New York.

Welsch, Wolfgang 1997, *Undoing Aesthetics*, Sage: London.

Tellef Kvifte

Digital Sampling and Analogue Aesthetics

Introduction

The concepts of "sampling", "digital", and, not least, the combination of the two concepts in "digital sampling" are ubiquitous in literature and discourse on music in the 21st century. Sometimes hailed as a revolutionary new creative principle, and sometimes dismissed as a technological monster that kills music and artistic expression in general, the concept of sampling is used in many ways for many different purposes.

Also, "digital" is used in many ways, and while many people seem to have grasped the meaning of the term as applied to sound technology, there seems to be no general understanding of what the term should be taken to mean when it comes to characterisation of cultural expressions or aesthetics. What should be implied by a term like digital aesthetics? One of the points I will try to defend in this chapter, is that digital *technology* does not in any real sense necessarily imply a "digital expression" or a "digital aesthetic", whatever one chooses to mean by such terms. If a piece of music is transmitted by means of a digitally based technology, it does not automatically become a digital musical expression. The interplay between the character of the cultural expressions and the underlying technology is complex, and it is not always obvious how to characterise technology that contains both analogue and digital components, as indeed all modern music technical devices do.

Also, I will try to show that the contemporary development of the so-called digital media technology in the field of music production is better understood as an *analogue* rather than as a *digital* revolution. The discussion of the concept pair analogue/ digital will therefore be an important part of this chapter.

I will discuss the concept pair analogue/ digital as a tool to characterise both the technological basis of old versus new media technology, as well as communicational and aesthetic expressions in different forms.

Also, I will discuss the occasionally pointed aversion to the "digital" and "digital media" that several authors voice – not because I want to defend the media, but because I believe the concepts are often used in ways that confuse our understanding of modern media and the communication going on with the use of these media.

As much of the debate will revolve around the concept of "digital sampling", it is convenient to start with a closer look at the concept of sampling.

What is sampling?

There are a number of different and distinct ways that the concept of sampling is used in the literature. Even if the meanings are quite different, it is not unusual to find them used almost interchangeably.

First of all, the concept of sampling is used to describe the core technology of contemporary sound production, that is, how sound is converted from the analogue to the digital domain. Here, "analogue" simply means "continuous", and "digital" means "discrete": A continuous signal is converted to a series of discrete symbols. In principle, this is a very simple and straightforward process: The amplitude is measured at regular intervals, and the values are stored in a list. This digitalisation – or "discretisation" if you like – is done in two dimensions. Measurements are done at discrete intervals in time and not continuously; further, each measurement is assigned one of the available discrete values (see Figure 1).

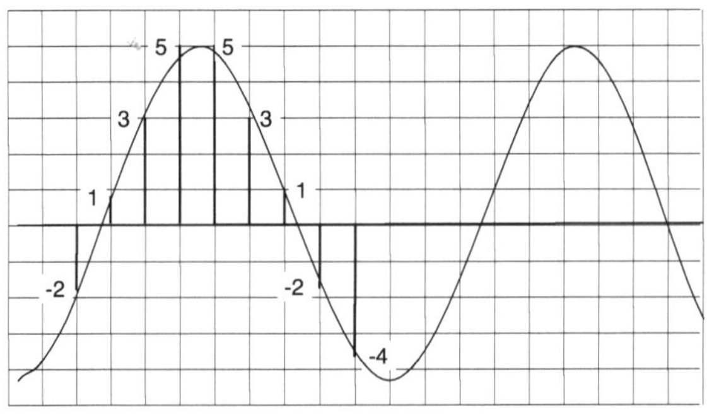

Figure 1. Sampling$_1$ - a continuous signal is measured at discrete intervals along a discrete scale.

Each such measurement is called "a sample" [1]. The list of measurements is a *digital representation* of the sound, and may be processed in a number of ways, including sending it through a so-called digital-to-analogue converter that will translate the digital representation back into the analogue domain, where it may be used to drive a loudspeaker so that we can (again) hear the sound. I will call this *$sampling_1$* when I need to distinguish it from the other meanings of the concept.

A second meaning of sampling (*$sampling_2$*) is used in connection with instruments called *samplers* that use recorded sounds to emulate or mimic the sounds of other instruments. Commonly, samplers are played by means of a keyboard, or controlled from some kind of music production software. In this connection, "a sample" refers to the recording of one single sound (a tone or a drum-hit). To make the sampler play a piano sound, for instance, one would normally use a large number of different samples, recorded at different pitches and at different volumes. The sampler will then play back the relevant samples, (possibly after some processing like transposing samples to the desired pitch) when a key is pressed on the keyboard, for instance.

A third way to use the concept of sampling – *$sampling_3$* – is to describe the process whereby a musician/ composer includes part of an earlier recording in his/ her own music, as a more or less recognisable citation. Here, "a sample" is a continuous part of an earlier recording, and may be very short (like a "sound" used in a sampler instrument), several seconds, or even minutes long.

Sometimes two or more of the three meanings discussed so far are used seemingly interchangeably, in a confusing way. For example, Katz writes:

> ... the practice of digital sampling, a form of musical borrowing in which a portion of one recording is incorporated into another... Digital sampling is a type of computer synthesis in which sound is rendered into data, data that in turn comprise instructions for reconstructing that sound. Sampling is typically regarded as a type of musical quotation, usually of one pop song by another, but it encompasses the digital incorporation of any prerecorded sound into new recorded work... (Katz 2005, p 137–138)

Here, $sampling_1$ and $sampling_3$ are almost fused in the discussion, not only by the close juxtaposition of the descriptions of them, but

[1] The standard for CD-quality sound is to take 44100 samples each second. Each sample is characterised by a resolution of 16 bits, meaning that there are 2^{16} or 65536 different values to choose from.

also by the misleading inclusion of the word "digital" in the expression "digital incorporation of any pre-recorded sound" – misleading, because there are also analogue forms of sampling$_3$, as even Katz himself discusses. This almost automatic inclusion of the term "digital" in connection with "sampling" is quite common, but in fact, of the three possible meanings of sampling described above, only the first is really unambiguously "digital", as it describes the actual process of digitalisation of a signal. Sampling$_2$ and sampling$_3$ are possible with both digital and analogue technologies, and are not in any way intrinsically digital *phenomena*, even if digital technology is the basis for almost all sampling tools today.

A few examples from recording practice

In the late 1970s, a traditional fiddler made a recording in a studio in Oslo. The recording was made directly on a two-track stereo magnetic tape. When it was decided which "take" to use, we all agreed that there was one motif in the first part of the tune that was not quite up to standard, and it was decided to make an edit. A copy of the same motif, as it appeared in the second part of the tune, was made on another tape, and then spliced into the tape where the first, not so good version, was. The cut is impossible to hear, even to those of us who were there when the editing was done. The process of copying one part of the tune and splicing it back in at another spot was one of several common editing techniques used during the analogue tape recorder era of sound recording. Even if it is not usually described in the literature as such, it definitely represents a kind of sampling; similar to sampling$_3$ as described above, here performed with strictly analogue equipment. While sampling$_3$ is supposed to be recognised, the opposite is true here – an edit is successful only if it is not noticed at all by the listener. Let us call this technique *sampling$_4$*.

Ten years later, in a well-known studio in Oslo, where a female singer is making her first international album: The recording is done on a 48-track digital tape recorder. In the recording process, all of the instruments and the singer were typically recorded at the same time, but with (at least) the singer being totally acoustically separated from the other musicians. The singer could, therefore, make a number of additional takes on separate tracks. The usual procedure was (and still is) to pick the best pieces from a number of different takes; sometimes large chunks like a complete verse, and sometimes quite small bits down to single syllables or notes. On one occasion during the mix, we were not able to find a good version of a certain word in any of the available takes. The singer had caught a cold, and a new take was therefore not an option. We then located the same word in another verse; made a digital copy of it in the digital memory of the digital tape recorder, and placed the copy on a new track at the relevant place. Here, an important part of the technical process was digital: the sound was stored in a digital format, and the copy and paste process was done on digital entities. This is an example of digital $sampling_4$. But the artistic process; the musical shaping of the musical material, is exactly the same as in the first example.

Going back a few years: in the mid 1980s, a group playing medieval music was making a recording in Oslo. The six-piece ensemble was recorded in a church, using only two microphones, and a two-track tape recorder. The two-microphone-technique put us into a recording situation quite similar to the earliest gramophone recordings, as the balance between the instruments had to be done by positioning the musicians in the recording room, rather than by setting levels on a mixing desk. There was no post-production, no mix, no balancing, no adding of reverb, no equalisation, no panning – and no way to make repairs. The artists felt this production process helped them to attain a certain authenticity in their expression. They definitely had no thoughts of using sampling, but the tape recorder happened to be a digital tape recorder, the music was recorded in a digital format, and in this sense, the whole recording was based on sampling.

Sampling as an artistic practice is far older than modern digital technology, and certainly far older than the examples from recording practice discussed here. Hugh Davies traces $sampling_2$ – sampler instruments – back to the Romans:

> The concept of one instrument that sounds like another is not a new one. In Roman times one of the oldest instruments, the hydraulis, the early pneumatically powered pipe organ, was expanded by adding separately controllable parallel sets of pipes (ranks) which were later to be identified by the names of other instruments whose timbres they most closely resembled, leading to the large multi-timbral instruments that were installed in many mediaeval European cathedrals. (Davies 1996, p. 4)

If this counts as an example of sampling, which is not unreasonable, as the artistic device is a parallel to modern sampler instruments, it certainly is not digital sampling in the modern sense.

One of the lesser known examples is a device based on gramophone recordings, patented in 1917[2] (see Figure 2). This (analogue) instrument was probably never built, but it shows that the idea of a sampler instrument is not a result of the digital age.

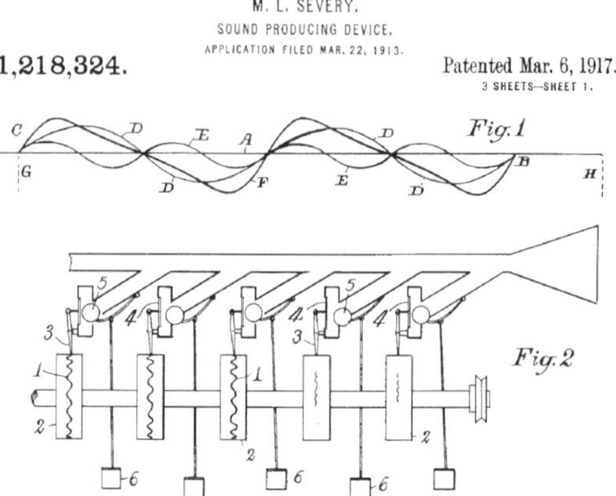

Figure 2. Illustration from sampler patent by Melvin L. Severy, granted 1917. A series of phonographic discs (2) are mounted on a revolving axis. The sound recorded on each disc can be played back by pressing the corresponding key (6). (U.S. patent nr 1218324.)

A more recent example of sampling$_2$ is the keyboard instrument Mellotron (Figure 3), where each key on the keyboard activated the playback of a tape recording of the corresponding pitch of an acoustic instrument, like a violin. This instrument was used on a number of recordings from the second half of the sixties, among them "Strawberry Fields Forever", where The Beatles used it for the flute intro. The tape technology in the Mellotron was analogue.

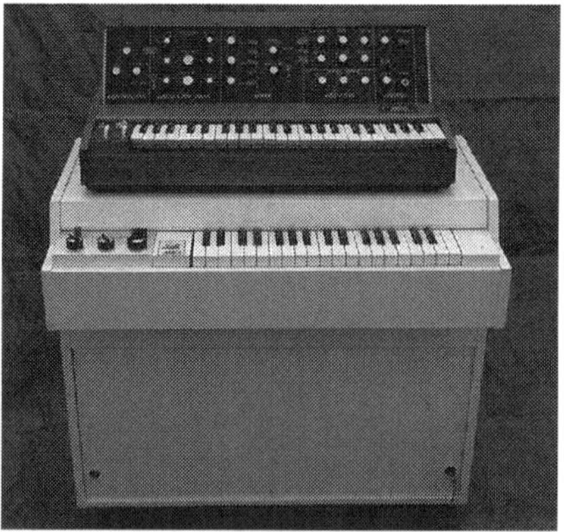

Figure 3. Mellotron, with a Minimoog synthesiser on top.

[2] Both this example and the Mellotron below, are mentioned in the Davis 1996 paper.

Turning to sampling$_3$, we also find that this concept may be seen in a longer historical perspective than that of digital music technology:

> As a form of musical borrowing, the roots of digital sampling reach back more than a millennium. Consider just the Western musical tradition: medieval chants freely incorporated and adapted melodic patterns from earlier chants; dozens of Renaissance masses were based on the melody of the secular song "L'Homme armée"; a similar craze raged centuries later when composers such as Berlioz, Liszt, Rachmaninoff, Saint-Saéens, and Ysaÿe "sampled" the chant Dies irae… (Katz:2005, p. 139)

Finally, sampling$_3$, the inclusion of recordings in a work of music, is of course also possible with analogue recordings, and the technique has been used with most available recording technologies since the invention of the wax cylinder. Also the repair technique of sampling$_4$ is fully possible with both analogue and digital means, as we have seen.

These examples are meant to show that there is no simple connection between digital technology and the practice of sampling. With the exception of sampling$_1$, all described versions of sampling may be carried out by either analogue or digital technology, and, on the other hand, the use of digital recording technology does not necessarily imply sampling as an aesthetic or artistic technique.

The concepts of analogue and digital in communication processes

Obviously, the term "sampling" is not applicable to the hydraulis in the same way as to modern sampler instruments, and it is equally obvious that the term "digital" is not applicable to the L'Homme armée -example in the same way as to taking a digital sound snippet from a recording and incorporating it into another. Even if Katz makes some effort to discuss the differences, he does not comment clearly on this core point: what "digital" is supposed to mean. As we shall see, there is more to it than sampling, and there is more to "analogue" than old technology.

The use of the analogue/ digital concept pair is relatively well-established in descriptions of technical processes, but the concepts are to a large extent overlooked as being useful to describe cultural expressions and practice. An exception is found in a rare and illuminating discussion in Davies' article on the history of sampling. He starts with the following observation:

> Most people are unaware that our current transition from analogue to digital technology is the second stage in a development that began around the middle of the last century, culminating in the mid-1870s. *Up to then all communications had been digital,* though not necessarily binary, for example the electric telegraph and Morse code as well as much older non-electrical systems like semaphore and Native American smoke signals. It was the virtual simultaneous invention of the telephone (Alexander Graham Bell) and the phonograph (Thomas Alva Edison) that ushered in a century of analogue technology. (Davies:1996l, p. 3) (my emphasis)

Here, we are reminded that "digital" is a concept that is not exclusively tied to the modern media situation. It seems also that Davies implies that the concept today tends to be used in a too narrow a sense, when it is used to refer exclusively to the kind of digitalisation described as sampling_1 above. Davies' use of the concept is wider, and is used to characterise how the communication system works as communication, and not only as technical construction. To Davies' examples of slightly exotic digital communication systems, one might add more familiar systems like the alphabet and standard music notation. This wider usage of the terms is developed by for instance Bateson (1968, 1972), Ruesch (1951) and Wilden (1980)[3]. For some reason, this tradition of communication research seems to be almost invisible in recent literature on digital media and aesthetics, even if the treatment of the central concepts of analogue and digital should also be quite relevant in the more recent discourse.

Like Davies above, writers in this tradition use the concepts to characterise *communication processes* rather than technical principles. Further, the concepts are used to characterise *aspects* of communication, that is, an act of communication is not necessarily either digital or analogue. On the contrary, both analogue and digital aspects are typically present in the communication, depend on each other in various ways, and take care of different layers or aspects of communicational content.

The basic and defining quality of digital communication is that it is based on discrete entities that are completely distinct. The letter "a" is distinct from all the others in the alphabet, and there is no meaningful gradual transition from "a" to "b". That is not to say that all aspects of a communication that uses the alphabet are digital. In handwriting, each instance of the letter "a" will be written slightly differently from the others, and my "a" will look different from your

[3] See also e.g. Hoffmeyer (2002) for application of the concepts in biology.

"a". What I communicate in the words I write, is a digital part of the communication; what I may communicate about my personality and emotions through my handwriting, is an analogue part. The words I speak are digital code; the way I speak is an analogue part of the communication. Also, in the actual performance of sending a message in Morse code, there is an analogue component – what we today might call the "micro-rhythmic variations" in shorts and longs, how the Morse code was sent – and this component is as good an identification of the telegraphist as the handwriting is of the writer.

This view is easily transferred to the performance of music[4]. Pitch may be regarded as a digital system as far as the ordering of pitches in scales and intervals are concerned. This is reflected in the representation of pitches in conventional music notation, with discrete symbols for each scale step. A scale step "c" is clearly distinct from "c-sharp", and there is no gradual transition from the "c-ness" of the c to the "c-sharpness" of the c sharp.

But there is also an analogue component of the experience of pitch. A "c" may be played out of tune, and the pitch may change gradually in a glissando or a vibrato. These are all *continuous* phenomena – a pitch may be more or less out of tune, but we have no discrete concepts for different degrees of "out-of-tune-ness". A similar argument may be made for rhythm, where one tends to classify durations of tones into a few classes – as also here reflected in the system of standard music notation – but the actual performance may be more or less "in time" with the supposed time values of the categories. One may perceive a musician as playing a distinct, classifiable rhythmic figure (digital), and at the same time experience the playing as slightly out-of-time, or as "groovy", "energetic" or "sloppy" etc (analogue).

The implications of analogue and digital

Bateson claims that analogue communication is to a large extent concerned with expression, relations and emotions. Given the examples of handwriting and speech, it is not difficult to see the point. One of Bateson's favourite examples is that when a person says "I

[4] I have also developed these concepts in relation to music in for instance Kvifte (1985, 1989).

love you" to another person; the other person will probably listen more to the way it is said than to the actual words, to decide what the words really mean.

Interestingly, there is a whole literature on "expressive timing" where the analogue aspects of rhythm are studied[5]. Keil's concept of "Participatory Discrepancies"[6] (commonly abbreviated "PDs") also falls in the same category, where minute analogue variations are seen as expressively important parts of the musical communication. To Keil, the (digital) communication that might be represented in a score, is seen as being concerned with structure and not with expression.

Furthermore, Bateson also claims that analogue communication is largely unconscious in our everyday communication. We may – consciously – think we pay attention to the factual content of a verbal statement, while we – unconsciously – pay as much, or more, attention to the way the message is conveyed, to the tone and expression, that tell us about our relationship with the speaker, what kind of power relation we have; what affective relationship we have, whether or not the speaker is to be trusted, etc. For Bateson, this is a key point, as he holds that the relational information usually is far more important, and for that reason, it is of survival value that we are not able to consciously modify this part of the communication, the implication being that a consciously constructed analogue message is not honest or authentic; in other words, it's cheating.

To what extent analogue communication is really on an unconscious level will obviously vary. Analogue communication is not *exclusively* about relations and emotion, nor are relations and emotions communicated exclusively by analogue means. As Wilden points out, the analogue and the digital serve different functions in communication, and "they seem always to be found together in all communication systems, and at every level of communication" (Wilden 1980, p. 168).

An example of this intimate relationship is found in rhythm perception[7]: the expressive, analogue variations of the PDs mentioned above have to be understood relative to a framework or a structure, that is, precisely the digital aspect of the music communication. Put in another way: if there is no reference, it is not possible to perceive anything as a variation. The same applies to the pitch perception, if

5 See for instance Bengtsson:(1974), Clarke (2000), and Kvifte (2004) for further references.

6 Keil (1994).

7 See Kvifte (2004) for a fuller discussion.

one is to (analogically) perceive a tone as out-of-tune, there has to be a fixed (digital) reference against which the tone may be compared.

An especially interesting view on vibrato in this connection is Katz' explanation of why vibrato in concert violin playing became much more prominent after the introduction of gramophone recordings:

> I would suggest that a constant and strong vibrato became increasingly useful for the concert violinist who regularly made recordings, and it did so in three ways. First, it helped accommodate the distinctive and often limited receptivity of early recording equipment. Second, it could obscure imperfect intonation, which is more noticeable on record than in a live setting. And third, it could offer a great sense of the performer's presence on record, conveying to unseeing listeners what body language and facial expressions would have communicated in concert. (Katz 2005, p. 93)

This is interesting to us both because Katz sees a clear connection between an analogue communicative act (the use of vibrato) and the expression of personality, but also because of the more general point that the very act of recording is an important factor in the aesthetic process.

It is in fact a truism in recording studios today that the standard of pitch precision is much narrower on a recording than in a live performance. Quite some effort – both in terms of recording time and in terms of post-recording "repair" – is put into avoiding unintentional pitch deviations. This is not only for some general aesthetic reason. Analogue pitch control is one of the really important ways in which a musician can communicate competence, and much attention is paid on getting this right. But it should be noted that this is independent of whether the technical basis of the recording is analogue or digital; this should be understood as an effect of the recording as such.

Sampling as aesthetic communication

Against a background of this wider meaning of analogue and digital, it becomes obvious that a term like "digital sampling" may be highly ambiguous, unless it is made clear whether one refers to the technical medium or to the communicational act.

The concept of sampling$_1$ is clear, however, because this concept refers exclusively to a technical process, and since the concept simply describes the process of digitalisation, it is obvious that "digital sampling" is the right description. The other cases are not that obvious.

Technically, both sampling$_2$ and sampling$_3$ may, as we have seen, be implemented as either digital or analogue, e.g. by the use of analogue magnetic tape technology or by digital computer technology. But regardless of the technology used in the sampling, there may also be communicational content coded analogically or digitally – or both.

Sampling$_3$ is a good case in point, at least if we follow Katz above, where both the inclusion of bits of musical notation from previous works, and the inclusion of recordings in other recordings are considered examples of sampling.

The inclusion of the musical notation of part of a work in the musical score of a new work, is, in the way the terms are used here, a clear example of *digital* sampling; the musical notation being a digital system of communication like the alphabet. Of course, during a performance of such a work, there will be analogue aspects like in any musical performance, but the sampling as such – the inclusion of a specific chunk of musical notation in a score – is done with a digital code. What is transferred from the other work through the sampling, is exclusively digital content, like pitch and duration classes; not any analogue information about e. g. precise timing and intonation.

If one includes a *recording of a performance* in another recording, it is strictly speaking both analogue and digital sampling, as both analogue and digital aspects of the performance are included in the process. Both the pitch and duration classes, as well as the way they are played, are transferred to the new context. One might nevertheless perhaps argue that the analogue aspects are at the centre of interest in this case, because if one wants to cite only the digital aspects, one might as well have played the citation instead of sampling it.

Is then a purely analogue sampling conceivable – the sampling only of 'the way it is played' without sampling any notes or durations classes? In other contexts than music it is common and obvious, in the form of imitation and parody. When an actor imitates a well-known person, it is the analogue aspects of speech – sound quality, inflections etc, and not the actual words that are imitated; the actor may very well use words that the person being imitated has never used at all, but nevertheless *sound* like the person in question.

The use of so-called "groove templates" discussed below may be seen as a parallel example of transferring analogue content, though usually without connotations of parody.

Also sampling$_2$ – the so-called sampler instruments – may, as the concepts of analogue and digital concepts are used here, be characterised as basically analogue. The reason is that this form of sampling is used to imitate the *sound qualities* of given instruments, that are basically modulated and conveyed by analogue parameters in the music, as will be further described below.

Digital technology and the return of the analogue

As I have argued here, what is commonly called "digital sampling" may, from an aesthetic point of view, often better be termed *analogue* sampling, because what the underlying digital technology makes possible is an increased aesthetic manipulation and control of the expressive analogue content of music. Following Katz above and the Dies Irae-example, we may even argue that purely digital sampling is not a new phenomenon, on the contrary, it is the technical possibility of analogue sampling that is the new aesthetic device that modern music technology has brought us. This is underlined by the fact that one of the most pronounced trends in the development of music software (and software instruments) in the last few decades is the many new ways to control the analogue aspects of music.

One example is the "digital sampler" – that is, the sampler$_2$ described above. It is called "digital" because the sound signal used in the instrument is digital; the illustration in Figure 4 takes this even a step further, since the whole instrument is made in computer software: the instrument itself is digitised.

Nevertheless, the instrument is geared towards controlling or manipulating the *analogue* aspects of music. The figure shows the part of the instrument where the setup is made; where the single samples (in this case single notes sung by a choir) are represented by rectangles in the field below the keyboard representation. This is a digital part of the set-up as discrete samples are assigned to discrete keys on a keyboard. All the knobs surrounding this area, however, may be used to alter and shape various analogue aspects of the sound – e.g. timbral aspects, analogue timing and pitch alterations – giving an extremely detailed control over the analogue aspects of the sound from the sampler. As is obvious from the figure, without going into details of each and every knob, there are many control parameters.

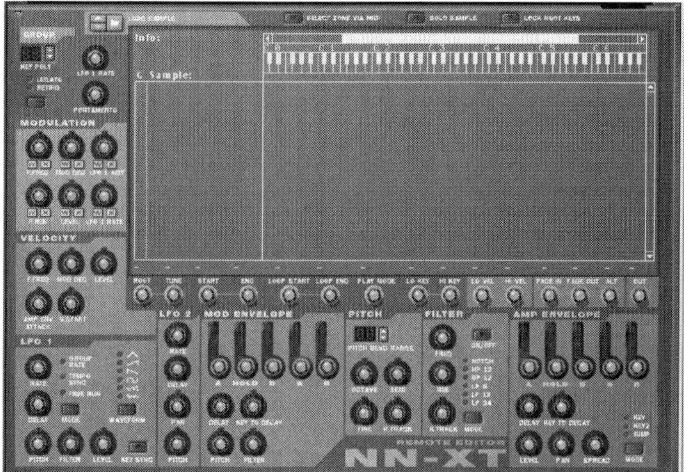

Figure 4. Control panel of a software sampler included in the software studio *Reason.*

Another example is from a software system called *Live*, where audio files of various lengths may be imported, and set to play back in various ways. The samples (as the imported audio files are called in this connection) may be played back as loops or just once at a time; one or more samples may be played at the same time, and the length, speed and pitch of the samples may be changed. One interesting window is shown in Figure 5. Here, the intensity graph of a sample is shown, and the program has added markers for what the program believes[8] are the four beats of a two-bar loop. A performer may grab any of these markers and drag to the right or to the left, and in this way indicate where in the sample s/he wants the indicated beat to fall. In this way, the performer has control over the analogue aspects of timing.

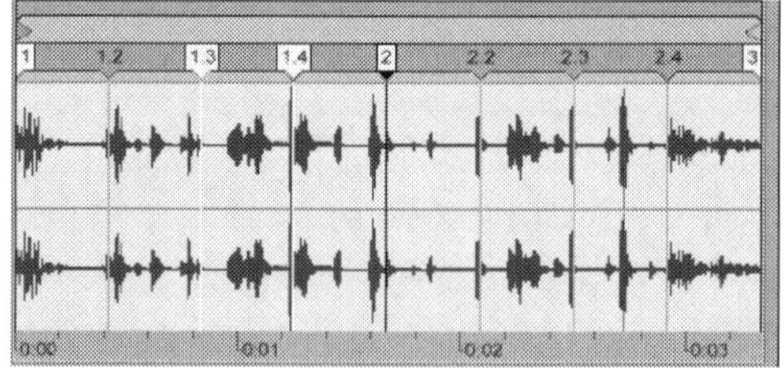

Figure 5. Loop manipulation in *Live.*

[8] A lot can be said about referring to software as acting agents, as I do here. Let me say that I use words like `believe' and other verbs only metaphorically in connection with software.

Techniques to analyse and extract the analogue timing from a short piece of music are found in several music production software packages. Figure 6 is taken from Logic Pro, and shows at the top the intensity graph of one bar of a recorded drum pattern. Below are three lines, essentially illustrating how the program builds a metric grid on the basis of the audio file and the metric structure chosen as basis for the analysis. The resulting "groove template" may then be used to shape other parts of the recording. One may, for example, play a melody on one track, and afterwards let it be "re-grooved" according to the pattern of the template to conform with the micro-rhythmic timing of a drum loop.

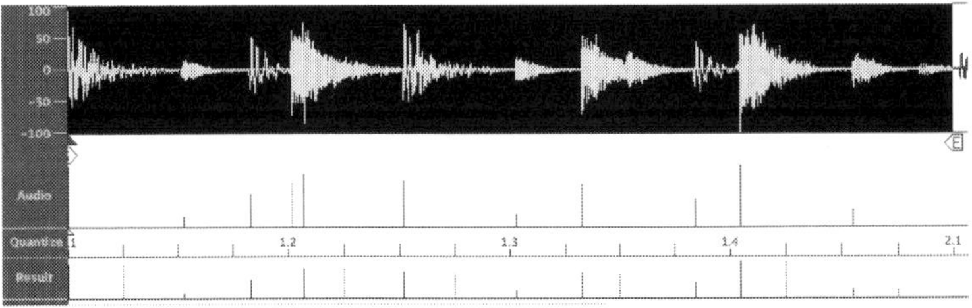

Figure 6. Analysis of `groove' in Logic Pro software.

Theses are just three examples (out of many possible) of how a digital technology is used to enhance the aesthetic control of analogue parameters. I also like to see the evolution in multi-track recording in the same light. Since multitracking became practical in the 1950s and in common use in recording studios during the 1960s, the number of available tracks has been a major selling point for studios. And the development from the 1980s when a 48-track digital recording machine would cost something like 150000 euros, till to-day, when one may have as many tracks as one can practically use available on a computer for the price of 1500 euros, clearly shows that multi-tracking has been considered a core technology of music production.

The main artistic reason for multi-track recording, with full separation of the instruments on the different tracks, is precisely to have as much control over the analogue parameters of music as possible. With the instruments totally acoustically separate from each other, sound, intonation and timing may be controlled (or manipulated, if you like) in great detail. Timbre may be adjusted; instruments may be accurately positioned in the aural space both right-left and front-back; intonation may be adjusted to make an instrument sound more in tune (or slightly out of tune to alter the overall timbre); timing may be adjusted to make the feel tighter or "ahead" or "behind" etc.

Therefore, if we are to understand the effects of the new technology, we should not only look at the properties and possible effects of *digital technology*, but even more at *analogue communication*. With the digital technology, the analogue has returned as the main focus of musical expression, in contrast to the historically, culturally and geographically relatively narrow period where the digital music notation was conceived as the main musical expressive instrument for the "real" musical creators called composers. If one should coin a term for what the digital technology means aesthetically, it should therefore not be a "digital aesthetic" but, on the contrary, an "analogue aesthetic" because what is really new in the aesthetic practice made possible by the new technology is the unprecedented creative control over the analogue aspects of the expressions.

I think this is a key point that has to be addressed in the ongoing debate on how to understand the new media. And there is more to it. The very concept "digital" has for many people strong connotations in the direction of "machine", "automatic", "not human" etc., while "analogue" has a much more human and authentic feel. I believe some of the concern about "sampling" and "digital sampling" that some authors have voiced is based on a conflation of "digital" and "machine", and partly also on an ignorance of the importance and functions of the analogue aspects of communication. In the final part of this chapter, we shall discuss this in more detail.

The problem of "the digital"

Given the (con)fusion of the different meanings of "sampling", as well as the concept of "the digital", it is no wonder that people often disagree over how to understand and value cultural expressions and aesthetic practices that are based on the new media technology. The opinions are often strong, like in this passage from Tara Rodgers:

> Andrew Goodwin frets over the increasing difficulty in distinguishing human- from machine-generated music and unleashes a barrage of incriminating descriptors of sample-based music, such as: 'orgy of pastiche', 'stasis of theft', and 'crisis of authorship' (Goodwin 1990: 260, 263, 270). He fails to acknowledge that sampling is a creative process, and that the so-called tactics of 'stealing' and 'pastiche' are musically and politically

> constructive, capable of encompassing a complex web of historical references and contesting dominant systems. (Rodgers 2003, 314)

This quote sums up some arguments from both sides of an ongoing controversy, a controversy that basically revolves around the question of whether digital media are good or bad. Even if Goodwin (1990) is neither the first nor the last to raise these questions, his paper is as good a place as any to take as a point of departure.

As Rodgers indicates in the quote above, one of the issues raised by Goodwin is what might be called "The problem of the machine". Goodwin lists four processes that he claims lead to "blurring distinctions between automated and human performance in today's pop" (264). Why this should be a problem, or why there is actually a higher level of confusion than earlier is not made very clear, and because Goodwin does not problematise the relationship between human and machine performance, the arguments never get beyond mere assertions. Let us have a closer look at the second process he describes:

> A second reason for the confusion is very simple. Much of today's technology allows musicians to play into the program, using drum pads, keyboards, or even buttons on the machine itself. This information will often register at very fine degrees of subtlety, encompasses parameters such as velocity and extremely small shifts in tempo and placement of the beat, and might trigger digital samples of "real" sounds that are indistinguishable from the originals. The result can be that the machine program contains every bit as much information as any piece of "real" playing. (Goodwin 1990, p. 264)

The situation described is actually of a musician playing, and recording the playing with the help of some kind of machine. What is the crucial difference between the situation described, and the recording onto magnetic tape of an acoustic instrument? Goodwin does not make any analysis of the central concepts, like "real playing", "instrument", "real sound" or "machine". What remains is a vague luddite argument that implies that there is something impure about machines used for making music.

Goodwin admits that the information content – probably understood as expressive content – is not degraded through the process described. Then we are left with two possible differences from a situation of live performance. The first concerns the "machine"; the other is the question of recording.

If the sound producing mechanisms of the machine is a problem, what exactly is the problem? First, we obviously accept many mechanical devices as legitimate sound producers in music-making, in the many forms of traditional acoustic instruments. The degree to which the performer is actually "producing the sound" varies a lot from instrument to instrument; sometimes such differences are discussed as relevant for e.g. how difficult instruments are considered to play for beginners, with clarinets and violins being considered as more difficult than e.g. a piano.

But the concept of "producing the sound" is not well-defined either. Consider first a singer: it is quite obvious that a singer produces the sound in all relevant ways of understanding the term. Moving to a piano, one may argue that there is a certain amount of mechanism between the performer's action of pressing a key, and the actual sound production when a hammer hits a string. Move on to a church organ, where there might be a considerable amount of mechanism between the performer and the sound-producing pipes; further, it may be argued that the performer has relatively little to do with how the sound is produced in a pipe, and not very much influence on the sound of each single organ pipe. We might continue with a synthesizer, and then go on to a traditional music box, where the performer does not do much more than winding a handle to get the instrument to produce a melody. It is not clear where on this continuum one should draw the problematic line between man and machine, and it may be argued that – possibly except for an open-air performance of un-amplified a cappella singing – there is *always* an element of technology involved in the production of music, whether the music is live, recorded, acoustic, electronic, or any combination of these. It also seems that there is no obvious qualitative breaking point along the continuum from no technology to a great deal of technology.

The example of the music box raises also the question of "automatic" as a category in the description of instruments, or in a wider sense, the question of agency. Who is doing what? Or, in Goodwin's context, does the musician do enough to be considered to be a musician? Actually, this is an extension of the previous question, and there is no clear distinction. In a way, it might be said that when a piano key is pressed, the piano automatically – by itself – makes the sound. But we normally do not use the term "automatic" here. A player piano, where tunes are programmed on a long paper sheet will, however, usually be considered "automatic". This is really an interesting case: take the modern parallel, MIDI-driven electronic instruments, or, to make the parallel even closer, a so-called *disclavier*. This instrument is really a standard, acoustic piano, with sensors and motors on each key on the keyboard. During a performance all the movements of the keys may be recorded. Afterwards, the movements of the keys may be played back to the motors, and this will activate the keys in the same way as the performer did during the original performance.

Consider a pianist playing a piece of music on such an instrument, and making a CD recording at the same time. Later, you may choose to play the CD recording of the performance, or let the piano play back the tune by reproducing the movements of the player. The latter case will – at least for some people – be considered an "automatic" performance made by a machine, while the CD recording will be considered a recording of a live performance, and not be "infected" by the machine in the same way. Why? In the case of the CD recording, the sound is bound to be poorer and further removed from the original performance than in the case of the automatic performance, that, for all intents and purposes, will be sonically indistinguishable from the original[9], and, in this sense, perhaps more "authentic".

I will not try to resolve the question of when music-making is to be considered mechanical rather than human; that is not my concern here. But it should be pointed out that the evidence from musical practice shows that where the line is drawn depends on social context and musical practice, and is more a result of the discourse and power negotiations among a group of music-makers and their audience, than it is a matter of logic or any objective properties of machines and man-machine relations.

I believe that one of the connecting points between questions of technology and questions of power is found in another of Goodwin's themes, namely what might be called "The problem of the originals." Goodwin refers, like so many others authors writing about "the digital", to Benjamin's concept of "aura", and claims that the

> Digital recording techniques now ensure that the electronic encoding and decoding that takes place in capturing and then reproducing sound is such that there is no discernible difference between the sound recorded in the studio and the signal reproduced on the consumer's CD system. This is something new: the mass production of the aura. (Goodwin:1990, p. 259)

This is perhaps the most widespread misunderstanding of digital technology. It is true that digital copies of material *already in the digital*

[9] Provided that the instrument is kept in tune and placed in the same room as the original recording was made.

domain are identical to the original. But to go from there to hold that there is no discernible difference between the *sound* recorded in the studio and the *signal* reproduced in the home of the listener is not only inaccurate, but sheer nonsense. First of all the concept of "the sound recorded" is highly imprecise. If this is understood literally, Goodwin disregards the highly important process of recording, and, not least, shaping the sound after the recording – the whole mixing and mastering process. And the sound that comes out of this process is of course vastly different from "the sound recorded in the studio".

If we understand the statement to mean the finished mix, there is still a big difference between what is heard in the studio, and what is heard in the homes of the listeners. Disregarding the obvious and important factor of room acoustics, one must note that the digital signal has to go through a digital-to-analogue converter; a piece of equipment that are made in a wide variety of qualities, and that affects the sound; from there the now analogue signal is passing through an amplifier that also may be of a very different quality and kind from that in the studio; finally the signal is sent through loudspeakers to be converted from an electric signal to sound. Loudspeakers in homes – not to speak of cars – are usually of a very different kind than those found in studios.

Thus, there is really no way that one can consider that the sound heard in the homes – as a result of the digital technology – is in any way so close to the studio sound as to be "identical", or to be sensibly called an "original". Therefore, it is hard to see why the digital technology, in contrast to analogue technology, should be able to transfer the "aura", whatever that is taken to mean. It seems that what Goodwin is really talking about, is not the aura Benjamin describes, but rather some kind of "negative aura" of the machines.

The roots of the unease at the digital

If there are no obvious reasons to condemn the digital technology on the basis of the problem of the machine or the problem of the original, what may then be the background for the attacks on the digital and on sampling?

I think one key is in the understanding of the new technology as being primarily important for analogue expressions. This has two important consequences. First, it is a profound break in relation to the mostly digitally oriented music-making of the musical notation. The change has several important consequences that mean shifts in power relationships on several levels. One such level is pointed out in connection with authorship; in my opinion not because authorship has in any way become unclear because of the digital technology, but because it is not obvious how to handle the shift of emphasis from digital music notation scores to analogue expressive content. What kind of role and status should be ascribed to e.g. studio technicians and producers that now have important roles in the analogue shaping of the musical products, not only in popular music, but in all kinds of musics that are distributed by way of recordings? One may also expect changes in connotations of words like "composer" and "performer", as well as in copyright systems.

The second important change has to do with education: the creative and aesthetic control of analogue parameters through contemporary music technology calls for skills very different from those needed to make music works in traditional music notation. There is no need to spell out in detail what kind of conflicts these question may lead to in education systems on all levels, and the quote from Tara Rodgers above is a good illustration on the almost paradigmatic differences of opinion we may find between the two sides in the controversy.

Is pitch correction cheating?

Finally, let us return to Bateson's views on analogue communication. A substantial part of the mixing process in a studio is concerned with shaping the analogue parts of the recording. One aspect concerns the relative strength and placement of the instruments in the sonic room. More important in this context, however, are the different techniques of "polishing" the sound and expression of each single performer. Apart from adjustments to the timbral qualities of the sound, one may also adjust, shape, or manipulate the precise timing and intonation of each performer; said in another way, "out-of-tune" as well as "out-of-time" singing and playing can be corrected under certain circumstances by more or less time-consuming techniques, and such procedures are part of the normal work in a recording. Is this cheating, or just a necessary work, following from the recording process itself? Considering Bateson's views on analogue communication, we should at least not be surprised that pitch correction is considered cheating by many as it will give the listener a false impression of the "real" competence of the performer[10].

Again, I will not try to resolve any conflicting views, and to really dissect the concepts involved is beyond the scope of this chapter. But it should be mentioned that to uphold a view of cheating in this connection, one has to somehow disregard the contemporary studio technology, either as pure malign technology, or at least as irrelevant for real music making. If, on the other hand, one regards the studio as a tool for making music, it is harder to dismiss the techniques sought and eagerly used by the creative staff involved in the production of music, as cheating.

Coda: Autonomous technology or aesthetics at work?

The contemporary, digitally based music technology has definitely changed the way music is made in many contexts. As I have argued here, the most profound change has to do with a shift of emphasis from the digital to the analogue aspects of music making. This shift is to a large extent made possible by the digital technology, but it is not, as artistic and aesthetic practices, *developed from* the digital technology.

As discussed, this shift has been under critique from a number of people, and I have tried to show that the perspective of analogue/digital as applied to the musical communication may be relevant to understand the ongoing debate.

There is a final point to be made regarding the unease connected to the contemporary music production technology that has to do with what is perceived as the driving force behind the change. Is it the technology as such, or are there aesthetic needs underlying it?

These are two very different perspectives to describe the situation. The one that I suspect is underlying some of the literature that describes the technology with unease is that the development is primarily a technological development; that development of the machines used has caused a change in the aesthetic practice of

---

[10] This is of course not to say that *Bateson* would consider this cheating.

music-making. Further, the change is perceived as irrelevant or even damaging to the real aesthetic needs of the artists. Such a view will fit in a long tradition of technology critics, where technology is seen as an autonomous force, developing by its own inner logic. Seen from this angle, we are witnessing technology at work in the change of aesthetic practice.

On the other hand, the great impact of the new technology may be viewed as an interplay between technological development and existing aesthetic practices – the needs of these practices driving a development of technology, resulting in new gadgets that in turn influence aesthetic practice. One of the main arguments underlying this chapter, is that increased aesthetic awareness of the analogue qualities is one important factor, and that this awareness has been stimulated by the possibilities of the core technology of multi-track recordings. This development started and got momentum during the era of analogue recordings, and would probably have been continued quite far by analogue technology if the digital sound recording and processing technology had not been made possible by the development of computer technology. Therefore, this should also be considered an example of aesthetics at work, where the artistic and aesthetic practices may be seen as important driving factors alongside the digital technology in the development of the field as a whole.

References

Bateson, Gregory 1968, "Information and Codification: A Philosophical Approach" in Ruesch, Jurgen & Bateson, Gregory (eds.), *Communication. The Social Matrix of Psychiatry*, W.W. Norton & Company, New York. pp. 168–211.

Bateson, Gregory 1972, *Steps to an Ecology of Mind.* Ballantine Books, New York.

Bengtsson, Ingmar 1974, "On notation of time, signature and rhythm in Swedish polskas", *Studia instrumentorum musicae popularis* vol. III, pp. 22–31.

Clarke, Eric F. 2000, *Categorical rhythm perception and event perception*, Keele University, Department of Psychology.

Davies, Hugh 1996, "A history of sampling", *Organised Sound* vol. 1, no. 01, pp. 3–11.

Goodwin, Andrew 1990, "Sample and Hold. Pop Music in the age of digital reproduction" in Frith, Simon & Goodwin, Andrew (eds.), *On Record: Rock, Pop and the Written Word*, London.

Hoffmeyer, Jesper 2002, "Code Duality Revisited", *Seed* vol. 2, no. 1, pp. 98–117.

Katz, Mark 2005, *Capturing sound: how technology has changed music.* University of California Press.

Keil, Charles 1994, "Participatory Discrepancies and the Power of Music" in Keil, Charles & Feld, Steven (eds.), *Music Grooves*, The University of Chicago Press, Chicago. pp. 96–108.

Kvifte, Tellef 1985, "Hva forteller notene? Om noteoppskrifter av folkemusikk." in Alver, Brynjulf (ed.), *Arne Bjørndals hundreårs-minne*, Forlaget folkekultur, Bergen.

Kvifte, Tellef 1989, *Instruments and the Electronic Age.* Solum Forlag, Oslo.

Kvifte, Tellef 2004, "Description of grooves and syntax/process dialectics", *Studia Musicologica Norvegica* vol. 30, pp. 54–77.

Rodgers, Tara 2003, "On the process and aesthetics of sampling in electronic music production", *Organised Sound* vol. 8, no. 3, pp. 313–320.

Ruesch, Jurgen & Bateson, Gregory 1951, *Communication. The Social Matrix of Psychiatry.* 2nd edn., W W Norton & Company.

Wilden, Anthony 1980, *System and Structure.* 2nd edn., Tavistock Publications.

Marius Wulfsberg

On Phototextuality

History, reading and theory

Recently there has been an increasing interest in the use of photographic images in literary texts. On the one hand a series of writers have published autobiographies, travelogues and novels where they combine text with pictures in new ways. On the other hand many critics have examined these interactions from historical, theoretical and hermeneutic perspectives, and discussed how our conceptions of writing and photography are transformed by their blending. An interesting consequence of these literary and critical explorations is the invention of the so called *phototext* and of related concepts such as the *phototextual* and *phototextuality*. In this essay I first present a short history of phototextuality which ends with a tentative definition of the term. Then I examine a selection of books from the phototextual tradition and identify what seems to characterise the interaction between text and photography. Finally I return to the introductory definition of phototextuality and elaborate on it.

A Short History of phototextuality

Ever since the invention of the daguerreotype in 1839, writing and photography have been crossing each others' borders. Their imbrications are already visible in the word "photography", which means "writing in light", and have unfolded in the specific works of a series of writers and photographers. When the American writer Edgar Allen Poe published the essay "The Daguerreotype" in 1840, he initiated a literary investigation of photography which was later continued by writers like Baudelaire, Strindberg and Ibsen. The investigation of the relationship between text and image seems to have become an important aspect of contemporary literature.[1] A parallel photographic investigation of literature can be traced back to the early photographer William Fox Talbot, who allied photography with literature by taking pictures of settings, landscapes and motives already described in the novels of Walter Scott, and thus initiated the photographic exploration of language which later has been developed by a series of photographers from Dorothea Lange to Sophie Calle.

At the end of the 19th century the first books which combined fictional prose and photographs appeared, and the novel *Bruges-la-Morte* by the Belgian writer Georges Rodenbach has become a reference point in the phototextual tradition. In the book the illustrations are an essential element in the literary work, and the motivation for them is explained by Rodenbach in the prefatory note. Nonetheless, it seems that the aesthetic awareness of the relationship between photography and writing became acute in the first part of the twentieth century, as the textual and photographic montages of Dadaism and Surrealism show. 1928 stands out as the year when the phototext became a part of modern literature. That year Virginia Woolf published the fictional biography *Orlando* which includes a series of painted and photographic portraits of the hero; and André Breton published *Nadja*, a book combining a written and a photographic report of his romance with a young woman. A theoretical instance of these phototextual montages can be found in Walter Benjamin's essay "A short history of Photography" (1931). The essay not only includes eight of the photographs commented upon, but the interaction between text and photographs is also treated theoretically. In his discussion of contemporary photography, Benjamin argues that the importance of captions and texts in our understanding of the photographic image is increasing. He claims that when the camera became sufficiently small, portable, and able to reveal previously secret and private images, extended captions were needed for the viewer to understand the picture, thus turning "all the relations of life into literature."[2] In 1939 the French writer Paul Valéry published the essay "The Centenary of Photography" where he looks back on the history of photography, and discusses its relation to literature. Where Benjamin observes a convergence of the text and the image, Valéry lays stress upon the difference between the photographic image of

---

1 See Jane M. Rabb 1996.
2 W. Benjamin 1980, 215.

reality and the literary transformation of reality into poetic figures, fictions and narratives. He argues that literary language begins where the photographic and historical documentation of reality stops. The domain of literature consists of "those components of the narrative or of the thesis that originate in the mind and are consequently imaginary, mere constructions, interpretations, bodiless things by nature invisible to the photographic eye [...]."[3]

The term "photo-text" was coined by the American photographer and writer Wright Morris to characterise the relationship between image and text in his books *The Inhabitants* (1946) and *The Home Place* (1948). When he returned to California from a journey around Europe in 1934, he began to write a series of short prose pieces. Eventually, he thought that with a camera he might photograph what he was attempting to capture in words. In a later interview he characterises the relationship between images and words in the photo-texts thus: "I do not have captions, but the facing text reveals the nature of the object that interests me: the life of the inhabitants whose shells they are, as Thoreau said."[4] A consequence of the collaboration between words and images in his work seems to be a certain fictionalisation, which I will return to, of the photographic image.

Later, the term "photo-text" was picked up and elaborated by critics and writers focusing on the relationship between photography and writing within literature as well as other cultural fields. In *Image and Word* (1987) Jefferson Hunter argues that the term *photo text* covers a range of authorial situations, and he mentions writers and photographers working together; writer and photographer brought together by an editor and so forth. The crucial point in his understanding of *the photo text* is the equal collaboration of the images and the words. Even if he points out that the photo text appears at the intersection between fiction and non-fiction, he argues that "it is in combinations of photography with nonfictional prose that the photo text achieves its fullest development."[5] In the anthology *Photo-Textualities* the editor Marsha Bryant argues that the photo-textual field can't be restricted to documentary texts and photographs, and instead she describes *photo-text* as documentary and fictional books which combine photographs and text in ways challenging what she calls the image/ caption model. This

---

[3] P. Valéry 1980, 195-196.
[4] M. Wright 1977, 148.
[5] J. Hunter 1987, 39.

model is criticised for restricting the collaboration between text and photographs to a form of dualism giving priority to either language or pictures. When the text functions as the valued term, photography is subordinated to the role of illustration; when the image functions as the valued term, the text is read as caption commenting upon the image. In contrast, the photo-text is characterised as a composite work where the photographs and the text interact with each other without the one being marginalised or subordinated to the other. She mentions a series of photo-texts from the American tradition, quotes theorists like Mary Ann Caws and Roland Barthes, and argues that the mutual interference of photographs and text involves a dialogue, which the reader and observer enters into and sponsors, and which with other dialogues forms part of a more general conversation. "Unlike the image/ caption model, the interference neither marginalises one textual component, nor draws rigid boundaries between literature and photography."[6] In the introduction to *Phototextualities* (2003) Alex Hughes and Andrea Noble point out that the main concern in theories of phototextuality is to examine the mutual interaction between text and photographs in historical, theoretical and hermeneutic perspectives, and thereby determine the changing functions of the phototextuality within different cultural contexts.

Today *the phototext*, *the phototextual* and *phototextuality* have become established terms in the literary and aesthetic research into the interaction between photography and language in literary works, as well as in their representations of a wide range of historical and political contexts. I have come across a definition of phototextuality in an essay by the Irish critic Johnnie Gratton which seems to point out the main features of the field. I will therefore end this short history of phototextuality by quoting and commenting upon it:

> As I propose to understand it here, the analytics of "phototextuality" assume a bifocal perspective. This perspective embraces, on the one hand, photographs, or at very least the idea of photography, as something textually under consideration and, on the other hand, a text or texts, or at least a possibility of text, as something triggered in or by photo. The term "phototextualities," again as I understand it, further implies a study of different kinds and degrees of relation that hold between image and language across a wide range of contexts.[7]

---

[6] M. Bryant 1996, 14.

[7] J. Gratton 2003, 182.

The definition consists of three components. First, the analytics of phototextuality presuppose a bifocal perspective which let the interaction between the text and the photograph appears in the first place. Second, this interaction implies that the photo in one way or the other relates to a specific text or to a more general concept of textuality, and the text in one way or the other relates to a specific photo or to the idea of photography. The challenge within the field of phototextuality is to determine how photographs relate to the text, and how the text is, as Gratton puts it, triggered by photographs. Finally, the definition indicates that the interaction between photographs and texts takes place within a wide range of cultural contexts, which also should be examined before the literary, photographic and cultural work of the phototext may be defined and determined.

Readings in the phototextual tradition

Following on from the background of this short history of phototextuality, I will now examine five books in the phototextual tradition, and sketch out what seem to be the most striking aspects of the interaction between image and words.

Bruges-la-Morte by Georges Rodenbach

The novel *Bruges-la-Morte* (1892) by the Belgian writer Georges Rodenbach consists of a written story and 35 half-tone reproductions of original photographs supplied by the Parisian image bank J. Levy and Co. and Neurdein Frères. The text tells the story of the widower Huges Viane, who still mourns the loss of his wife five years after her death. He has moved to Bruges, as he finds the town perfectly adjusted to his melancholy. Every day, he walks around the city seeking analogies of his sorrow in the canals and buildings, and by the narrative the city is transformed into an image of his dead wife. "Bruges was his dead wife. And his dead wife was Bruges."[8] One day, however, he gets a glimpse of a woman, the actress Jane Scott, who resembles his dead wife almost perfectly. A liaison between the widower and the actress develops until Hughes strangles her with a golden braid of his dead wife's hair. This fictional story is illustrated

---

[8] Rodenbach 2005, 33."Bruges était sa morte. Et sa morte était Brugess." (Rodenbach, 1998, 69).

by photographs without captions which show us views of canals, buildings, places and objects mentioned and described in the text. The images are placed on the page opposite where they are mentioned or very close by. Two examples: The opening photo, which shows a view of a canal leading into the centre of the city, corresponds to the textual description of Viane leaving his apartment for an afternoon stroll along the canals; the textual description of how the façade of his apartment at Quai du Rosaire is mirrored in a canal, corresponds to the photograph of the Quai du Rosaire a few pages later. This kind of phototextual interaction continues throughout the book, and transforms the reading of the text. As Paul Edwards has observed, the reader not only looks "at the photographs on the right, but also search for series of images of any location once it has been named", and once aware of the interaction between the text and the photographs, the reader often leaves off reading, skipping back and forth before pursuing the narrative.[9] This reproduction of the opening page of the novel might give an impression of the interaction:

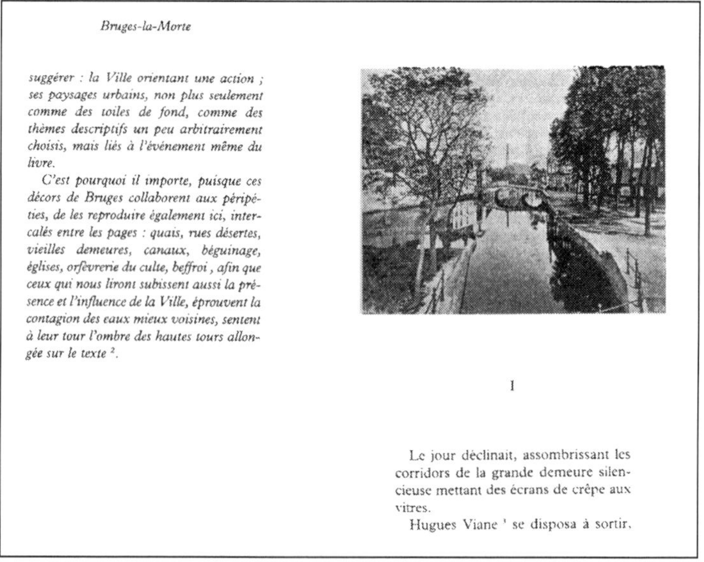

Bruges-la-Morte

suggérer : la Ville orientant une action ; ses paysages urbains, non plus seulement comme des toiles de fond, comme des thèmes descriptifs un peu arbitrairement choisis, mais liés à l'événement même du livre.

C'est pourquoi il importe, puisque ces décors de Bruges collaborent aux péripéties, de les reproduire également ici, intercalés entre les pages : quais, rues désertes, vieilles demeures, canaux, béguinage, églises, orfèvrerie du culte, beffroi , afin que ceux qui nous liront subissent aussi la présence et l'influence de la Ville, éprouvent la contagion des eaux mieux voisines, sentent à leur tour l'ombre des hautes tours allongée sur le texte [2].

I

Le jour déclinait, assombrissant les corridors de la grande demeure silencieuse mettant des écrans de crêpe aux vitres.

Hugues Viane [1] se disposa à sortir,

Figure 1. Reproduction of page 51 in the French 1998-edition.

In the prefatory note, Rodenbach presents what may be the first poetics of phototextuality in which he explains the motivation for the

[9] P. Edwards 2000, 73.

use of photographs by pointing out their relation to the fictive story, its urban environment and the reader:

> This is what we have tried to suggest: the Town guiding the action, its urban landscapes not merely as backcloths, as the slightly arbitrary subjects of descriptive passages, but tied to the very events of the book. That is why, since the scenery of Bruges is directly involved in the story, it is important that they should be reproduced here, interpolated between the pages – *quais*, deserted streets, old houses, canals, the *Béguinage*, churches, liturgical objects, the belfry – so that our readers, too, may come under influence of the Town itself, experience for themselves the shadows cast over the text by the tall towers.[10]

Three points seems to be important in Rodenbach's explanation of the use of photographs. First, it is motivated by the relationship between literary descriptions and the described reality. This relationship is often arbitrary, Rodenbach indicates, since the described environment is traditionally reduced to a backdrop or background. In this novel, the relationship between the place and the fictive story is closer; the action is guided by the Town of Bruges. Second, the intimate relationship between the urban landscape and the action can't be created by language alone, and that is why the photographs become important. They reproduce the scenery, the *quais*, the streets, the canals, the towers and churches. Thus the photographs make up for a certain lack in literary language and descriptions, i.e. the slightly arbitrary relationship between words and the referent, by making the places in the story visibly present for the reader. Third, the photographic images of the Town transform the reading of the text, since the fictional story and its atmosphere is accessible not only through the reader's decoding and interpretations of the text, but also through the photographs which are traces of the described reality and the urban landscapes.

One consequence of this interaction is that the photographs document the fictional story, and the text fictionalises the photographs.

---

10 G. Rodenbach 2005, 21. "Voilà ce que nous avons souhaité de suggérer : la Ville orientant une action ; ses paysage urbains, non plus seulement comme des toiles de fond, comme des thèmes descriptifs un peu arbitrairement, mais liés à l'événement même du livre. C'est pourquoi il importe, puisque ces décors de Bruges collaborent aux péripéties, de les reproduire également ici, intercalés entres les pages : quais, rues désertes, vieilles demeures, orfèvrerie du culte, beffroi, afin que ceux qui nous liront subissent aussi la présence et l'influence de la Ville, éprouvent la contagion des eaux mieux voisines, sentent à leur tour allonges sur le texte." (Rodenbach 1998, 49-50)

The Bruges we see on the photographs is not only the real, historical Bruges, but the photographs also become images in the fictional story. The interactions transform the Town into images of the protagonist's melancholy and a series of analogies arise between the textual descriptions of the protagonist and the photographs. The photographs complement the referential function of the fictional text, and the text fictionalises the reality imprinted on the photographs. Another consequence is that the reader becomes aware of the difference between the photographs and the text. As Edwards as well as other critics have observed, the photographs are related to the protagonist's experience of the past as a lost time beyond recovery. "The photographs are not there to call forth memories of Bruges to those who have visited the town. The novel does not situate the town in its economic context nor in its historical present, but in an indefinable past."[11] Even if the photographs depict places and objects mentioned in the text, the photographic images never becomes synchronous with the events of the fictional story. Thus the novel seems to explore three important aspects of phototextuality, namely the appearance of the temporal difference between the text and the image, the accentuation of the referential function of fictional language, and the fictionalisation of the photographic image and the reality it depicts. In the following we will see how other books in the phototextual tradition rearticulate these aspects and thus transform the field of phototextuality.

Nadja by André Breton

With the publication of *Nadja* (1928) Breton continues the phototextual tradition initiated by Rodenbach's novel, and the book has become a decisive reference point, both in the French and Anglo-American traditions.[12] However, *Nadja* is a text without a definitive genre, and it blends elements of the autobiography, the diary and the novel in its depiction of a series of real events that have taken place in the life of Breton. What kind of book is *Nadja*? In the opening lines Breton tells his readers that *Nadja* is one of those "books left ajar, like doors."[13] The first part consists of a series of anecdotes where Breton describes how he by chance met other surrealists like Benjamin Peret, Paul Eluard

---

[11] P. Edwards 2000, 84. See also D. Grojnowksi 2002, 93-120, and G. Rodenbach 1998, 7-44.

[12] See M. Wareheim 1996 and D. Grojnowski 2002.

[13] A. Breton 1999, 18.

and Robert Desnos. Then in the second part he relates in the form of a diary how he by coincidence got a glimpse of a young woman walking about in the streets of Paris on October 4, 1926 and got to know her. Their relationship develops into a love affair which culminates in an erotic scene eight days later, and through the eyes or perspective of the narrator Breton Nadja is transformed into a figure of the surrealistic being. In the last part of the book she has become mad and is admitted to a mental hospital, their liaison ends, and Breton reflects upon the relation between madness, love, beauty and surrealism.

The narrative is accompanied by more than forty photographs of places, people and art objects mentioned in the text and by some of the drawings Nadja did during her relationship with Breton. The photographs are taken by different photographers like J.-A. Boiffard, Man Ray and Henri Manuel, and the most striking aspect of the photographs is their seemingly plain realism, as this reproduction of the first picture in the book exemplifies:

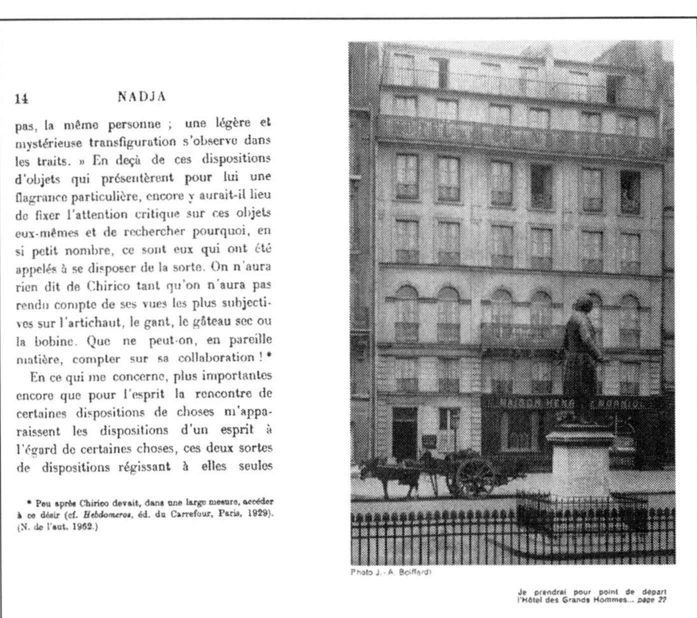

14 NADJA

pas, la même personne ; une légère et mystérieuse transfiguration s'observe dans les traits. » En deçà de ces dispositions d'objets qui présentèrent pour lui une flagrance particulière, encore y aurait-il lieu de fixer l'attention critique sur ces objets eux-mêmes et de rechercher pourquoi, en si petit nombre, ce sont eux qui ont été appelés à se disposer de la sorte. On n'aura rien dit de Chirico tant qu'on n'aura pas rendu compte de ses vues les plus subjectives sur l'artichaut, le gant, le gâteau sec ou la bobine. Que ne peut-on, en pareille matière, compter sur sa collaboration ! *

En ce qui me concerne, plus importantes encore que pour l'esprit la rencontre de certaines dispositions de choses m'apparaissent les dispositions d'un esprit à l'égard de certaines choses, ces deux sortes de dispositions régissant à elles seules

* Peu après Chirico devait, dans une large mesure, accéder à ce désir (cf. *Hebdomeros*, éd. du Carrefour, Paris, 1929). (N. de l'aut. 1962.)

Photo J.-A. Boiffard)

Je prendrai pour point de départ l'Hôtel des Grands Hommes... *page 22*

Figure 2. Reproduction of page 20–21 in the 1963-edition.

The main function of the photographs thus seems to be to document the narrative by making the places, objects and people that are mentioned visible for the reader of the text. This documentary function is even more explicit in the 1963 edition of the book, where Breton explains in the foreword that the photographs "eliminate all descriptions".[14] Maurice Blanchot describes the relationship between the narrative and the photographs thus in the essay "Tomorrow at Stake":

> What occurs in the narrative has occurred in actual fact. Something takes place there that took place at a time sometimes specified by a date (as one tears a page from a calendar) and in places photographs render present (while withdrawing them from verbal fluctuation). The narrative excludes fiction [...].[15]

However, even if the photographs eliminate or reduce the fictional elements of the textual narrative by documenting that the places, persons and objects mentioned in the text are real, it seems to me that the fictional and the literary re-appear on the level of the referred context. Or to be more precise, by including a set of photographs in the text, they not only refer to the context of the narrative, but they are turned towards the textual and narrative presentation of the events, and thus are transformed into a kind of documentation of Breton's experience of recounted events. For instance, the photograph above is not only a picture of L'hôtel des Grandes Hommes in Paris, where his story begins, but the different elements in the image becomes integrated parts of his surrealist text. There is one particular detail that stands out as decisive, namely the woman standing in the open window on the third floor. The woman is, in fact, the first image of Nadja in the text, pointing towards Breton's meeting with Nadja later on in the text. I don't claim that the woman in the photograph actually is the woman Nadja, but through the perspective of the narrator and protagonist Breton she is transformed into a figure of Nadja, and the surrealistic woman she represents in the text. A similar interaction between the literary perspective in the text and the photographs recurs in almost every photograph included in the book with the consequence that their seeming realism is transformed into a kind of documentation of the surrealistic experience of the reality described in the book.

---

[14] A. Breton 1988, 645.

[15] M. Blanchot 1993, 413. "Ce qui s'y passé s'est effectivement passé. Quelque chose a lieu qui a eu lieu dans un temps parfois precise par une date (comme arrache une feuille à un calendrier) et dans des endroits que les phototgraphies rendent presents (en les soustrayant à la fluctuation verbale). Le récit exclut la fiction [...]." (M. Blanchot 1969, 606).

At the end of the book, Breton even comments upon this interaction between the textual narrative and the photographs thus:

> I have begun by going back to look at several of the places to which this narrative happens to lead; I wanted in fact – with some of the people and some of the objects – to provide a photographic image of them taken at the special angle from which I myself had looked at them. On this occasion, I realised that most of the places more or less resisted my venture, so that as I see it, the illustrated part of *Nadja* is quite inadequate [...].[16]

Precisely the inadequate relationship between the text and the photographic images seems to be the very reason *Nadja* is regarded as an important work in the phototextual tradition. In the book the photographs do not exactly complement the fictive story, but instead there is a certain resistance and difference between the "the illustrated part" and the written narrative, between the photographic images of places and objects, and the angle from which the narrator and protagonist André Breton looks at them. This inadequate relationship seems to have haunted Breton himself, who, in 1963, published a new version of the book where the illustrated part is changed and expanded. In the later version the new photographs have been taken from an angle closer to that from which the protagonist and narrator looked at the depicted persons and objects, but without eliminating the resistance of the places and people. In the book there are, I will argue, two levels of interaction between the text and the photographs. First the photographs documents the written narrative and force us to read it as a nonfictional text referring to a series of real events; second the photographs and the text document how the fictional and the literary is at work in the reality depicted in the book. The interaction creates an ongoing motion between the real and the surreal.

The Home-Place by Wright Morris

Wright Morris not only seems to be the inventor of the term "phototext", but his combination of photographs and text in his photo-texts

[16] A. Breton 1999, 152. "J'ai commencé par revoir plusieurs des lieux auxuels il arrive à ce récit de conduire; je tenais, en effet, tout comme de quelque personnes et de quelque objets, à en donner une image photographique aui fût prise sous l'angle spécial dont je les avais moi-même considérés. À cette occasion, j'ai constaté qu'à quelque exceptions près ils se défendaient plus ou moins contre mon entreprise, de sorte que la partie illustrée de *Nadja* fut, à mon gré, insuffisante [...]." (A. Breton 1988, 746).

as well as in his autobiographies, represents an important contribution to its history and development. To be more precise, his photo texts seem to have reduced the photographic resistance to the textual and literary transformation to a minimum. As I will argue, in his books the photographs are seen from the perspective of the fictional narrator and protagonist.

Morris published two phototexts, *The Inhabitants* and *The Home Place*, and then he began to write novels without photographs, because, as he puts it in an interview, "[t]he photo-text confronted me with many [problems]."[17] In later books like *God's Country and my People* (1969) he returned to the photo-text again, and in his many autobiographies he continued his exploration of the interaction between image and text, fiction and documentary. His critic Timothy Dow Adams describes these texts thus: "Not only does he put his fictional prose into his nonfictional autobiography, but he also uses his ostensibly nonfictional photographs within his novels in the form of both physical reproductions and prose descriptions of actual pictures."[18] In Morris' work there is a close relationship between the text and the reproduced photographs. Not only are the photographs taken by Morris himself, but they are also included in the books without captions. The text on the facing page often refers to and, as Adams points out, sometimes describes and interprets the reproduced image. This interaction is strengthened by the fact that Morris uses the same photographs in different books, and the photographs are taken and cut in ways that seem to refer to the context rendered present by the text. In Morris' phototexts the photographs are less the imprints of pieces of reality than cut-outs and pieces of the reality expressed by the text. Thus the text is motivated by supplementing the images, and when the photographs are included in the fictional text they are transformed from imprints of reality to imprints of the literary and fictional universe created by the text.

Let us take a look at the interaction between the first photograph and the opening of the narrative:

[17] W. Morris 1977, 148.
[18] T. D. Adams 2000, 177.

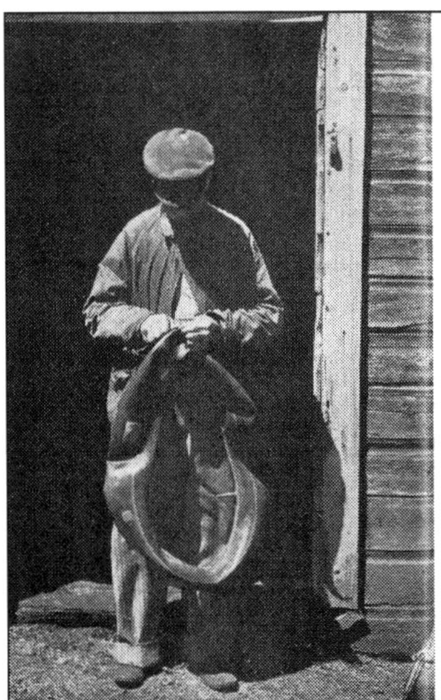

THE HOME PLACE

"WHAT'S the old man doing?" I said, and I looked down the trail, beyond the ragged box elder, where the old man stood in the door of the barn, fooling with an inner tube. In town I used to take the old man's hand and lead him across the tracks where horses and men, little girls, and sometimes little boys were killed. Why was that? They didn't stop, look and listen. We did.

"Is he planting melons?" Clara said.

"No, he isn't planting melons," I said. Clara put her hand over her glass eye, drew down the lid.

"If he isn't planting melons it would be nothing useful," she said.

"He's fixing his inner tube," said the boy.

"Thanks son," I said, and put my hand on his head. After the girl I wanted a boy so I could stand with my hand on his head, or his shoulder. But you can't. Try it sometime. I took my hand off his head and put it on the cool handle of the dipper, pressed on the handle, and skimmed off three drowned flies. I showed them to the boy and said, "Sprinkle them with salt and they'll be as good as new ones."

"How's that?" said Clara.

"I was just telling the boy to feed flies like that to the chickens." I opened the screen, and tossed the water into the yard. Four or five seedy leghorns ran through the shadows, scratched for them. "You see that, son?" I said.

"I told him to bring fresh water," she said, "but I don't think he's got around to it. He's eighty-one. He don't get around too much."

"You're not so young yourself," I said.

"I'm a farmer's wife," she said, and pulled a green stocking cap low on her head. My Aunt Clara is a raw-boned woman, a little over six feet tall, flat as a lath, and with the stalking gait of a whooping crane. In the early morning she wears a bright green stocking cap. She's been doing that for at least thirty years —against the night air, as she calls it—the tassel dangling over the

1

Figure 3. Reproduction of photo and page 1.

We see an elderly man standing in front of a door of a barn. He is holding an inner tube of a wheel in his hand and seems to be fixing it. The facing text begins thus: "'What's the old man doing', I said, and I looked down the trail, beyond the ragged box elder, where the old man stood in the door of the barn, fooling with an inner tube."[19] The first thing to notice is that the text begins by questioning what we see on the photograph. Even though the question is answered, it is the first signal of the close link between the photographs and the text. The text refers the reader to the image and vice versa. We also notice how the interaction between the text and the photographs transforms our way of looking at the photographs and of reading the text. The last thing to notice is the status of the "I" who poses the question. Later on in the text, we learn that his name is Clyde Muncy, and that he is visiting his home town with his wife and two kids, and the return to his home after thirty years in Chicago makes him wonder who he is: "Put it this way – for a moment I wondered who I was."[20] What challenges our understanding of the photographs is that they do not depict the views seen by Wright Morris during his visit to Nebraska

[19] W. Morris 1948, 1.

[20] W. Morris 1948, 20.

in May and June 1947, as the note on the photographs informs us, but they depict the views seen by the fictional protagonist and narrator. While he is looking at the views shown in the photographs, he wonders who he was and who he has become. The opening of the book is not the only place where the photographs show what the fictional character sees; this is the case throughout the book.

Thus the photographs in the phototext seem to document the imaginary universe constituted by the fictional text, and the distinctions between fiction and reality are set in motion in ways pointing towards later experiments with and definitions of the phototext. The bifocal perspective of the phototextuality which, according to Gratton's definition, embraces on the one hand photographs under textual consideration, and on the other hand texts triggered by a photo, results in an interaction where the photographs document the fiction of the text, and the text fictionalises the cut-outs of reality in the photographs.

Camera Lucida by Roland Barthes

Roland Barthes has a decisive position in the phototextual tradition both as a theorist and as a writer, and his main contribution to this field, *Camera Lucida*, may be regarded both as a theoretical and a literary phototext. The book can be read simultaneously as a theoretical, autobiographical and literary reflection on photography. Its subtitle is "Reflections on Photography", and the book is composed of 48 written paragraphs and 25 photographs divided into two parts. The first part is primarily written as a theoretical or a phenomenological investigation into the specificity of photographic images, where Barthes develops analytic distinctions like the *studium* and the *punctum* and establishes a theoretical perspective. In the very last paragraph of part one he suddenly dismisses his project of defining the essence of the photographic image, and the second part is introduced as his palinode of his argument thus far. Palinode is a Greek term which means "singing again", a discourse repeating an earlier one. In the second part, Barthes searches for the specificity of the photographic image in himself, and this descent into himself signals a kind of autobiographical turn as well. The second part opens with a description of a November evening when, shortly after the death of his mother, he looks through some photographs, and suddenly find a photograph of his mother as a six year old child, and in this photograph from the Winter Garden, he re-finds his mother. However, what particularly interests me here is not the description of the photograph of his mother as child in the Winter Garden, but the link between the photograph, which reveals the essence of photography for Barthes, and the text. Interestingly, the photograph of the mother is not reproduced in the text, because we, the readers, according to Barthes, will find nothing in it except its cultural and historical significance.

The various photographs in *Camera Lucida* maintain very different relations to the text. First, there are the textual commentaries of the photographs where Barthes points out the details which fascinate him, and thus makes the reader aware of what the writer sees in the photographs and how these details are theorised by the conceptual distinction between studium and punctum. Second, the reproduced photographs are furnished with captions which consist of excerpts from the text. More often than not the captions try to verbalise and pinpoint not the cultural significance of the photographs, i.e. the studium, but the details which suddenly strike him as fascinating, i.e. the punctums. Third, both the text and several of the reproduced images seem to refer to the photograph of the mother as a child in the Winter Garden, which reveals the essence of photography that the other images only indicate. In his analysis of *Camera Lucida*, Grojnowski discuss these different interferences between the images and the text and how they disseminate meanings. He argues that the interaction between the reproduced photographs, the captions and the text produces a series of different meanings while the unreproduced photograph of the mother is located *outside language*.[21]

In his analysis Grojnowski has a tendency to describe the interaction between the text, the reproduced photographs and the unreproduced photograph of the mother as a kind of mysticism. In my reading, the interaction may be explained by taking a closer look at the argument in Barthes' notes on photography. What constitutes the photographic image according to Barthes is that photographs prove the "having-been-there" of the subject, its past existence: "Contrary to these imitations [painting and language], in Photography I can never deny that *the thing has been there*. There is a superimposition here: of reality and past."[22] In other words, what constitutes the

[21] "Car loin de se prêter à la polysémie, elles tiennent le langage verbal en échec. Ce qu'elles manifestent ne procède pas des mots et apparaît, pour cela meme, dépositaire de l'essentiel." (Grojnowski 2002, 309).

[22] R. Barthes 1994, 76. "Au contraire de ces imitations, dans la Photographie, je ne puis jamais nier que *la chose a été là*. Il y a double position conjoint: de réalité et de passé." (R. Barthes 1980, 120).

photographic image according to Barthes is the referent. Language on the contrary is fictionalised and can never obtain the relationship to the referent of the photographic image:

> No writing can give me this certainty. It is the misfortune (but also perhaps the voluptuous pleasure) of language not to be able to authenticate itself. The *noeme* of language is perhaps impotence, or, to put it positively: language is, by nature, fictional [...].[23]

The interaction between photographs and text in *Camera Lucida* both theoretically and literary seems to establish an irreducible difference between the two forms of representations. While photographs are imprints of reality which beyond any doubt prove the "having-been-there" of the subject, language is fictionalised and its relation to the context and the reality is always problematic, a result of interpretation and cultural decoding. Against the background of my readings in the phototextual tradition, Barthes seems to articulate theoretically the differences between photography and language which Rodenbach indicates in *Bruges-la-Morte* and which provide Breton's poetic motivation for the use of photographic images in *Nadja*. As I have shown, Rodenbach argues that language establishes a kind of arbitrary link to the context of the fictional story while the photographs make them present even for the reader; and, according to Breton, the photographs eliminate every description and thus transform the book from a literary work to a non-fictional report from a surrealistic world. In *Camera Lucida* we learn that the photographic image is an imprint of a reality of "having-been-there" while any linguistic sign is fictionalised in the sense that it needs to be decoded and interpreted before it can refer to a given context. If *Camera Lucida* is often referred to as a decisive contribution to the field of phototextuality, the main reason is Barthes' realistic theory of photography in which the reference and the temporality of photography imbricate: reality and past. The distinction between fiction and reality which can be found in the earlier phototexts I have examined is given a temporal turn by Barthes. This temporal turn accentuates the relationship between image, memory, text and fiction, and seems to stand in the very centre of contemporary phototexts, like Paul Auster's *The Invention of Solitude* (1982), W. G. Sebald's *Austerlitz*

---

[23] R. Barthes 1994, 88-87. "Cette certitude, aucun écrit ne peut me la donner. C'est le malheur (mais aussi peut-être la volupté) du langage, de ne pouvoir s'authentifier lui-même. Le noème du langage est peut-être cette impuissance, ou pour parler positivement: le langage est, par nature, fictionel [...]." (R. Barthes 1980, 134).

(2001) and Orhan Pamhuk's *Istanbul* (2005), to mention just a few. I will therefore end this reading in the phototextual tradition, by an examination of the play of phototextuality in the autobiographical novel *Teori og praksis* (*Theory and praxis*) by the Norwegian writer Nikolaj Frobenius.

Teori og praksis by Nikolaj Frobenius

Teori og praksis is a novel which explore in a remarkable way the relationship between fiction and reality, and at the very centre of this investigation we find the interaction between text and photographs. The historical pretext for the novel is the author's childhood, but by its subtle structure and the challenging combination of text and photographs it sets the difference between the historical context and the fictional text in motion. The story begins in 1972, when the seven year old Nikolaj moves from the satellite town Ammerud to the newly build satellite town Rykkinn; and it ends when he leaves the town at the beginning of the 1980s. During these years Rykkinn is transformed from a social-democratic idyll to a dystopia. The young Nikolaj has become Niko the destroyed, his beloved mother is dead, and his father has lost all his illusions of the social community he thought the satellite town would create. When driving towards Oslo at the end of the story, Nikolaj observes that the world has been turned upside down and nothing is the same as it once was.

Teori og praksis is a novel, but the genre description has a footnote where the narrator discusses where the autobiography ends and the novel begins, and explicitly presents the book as an exploration of the border between non-fiction and fiction. How does the text answer or respond to this question? Where and how can the distinction between non-fiction and fiction be drawn in this book? The story paraphrased above is framed by a prologue and an epilogue both dated December 2004, and together they form an almost continuous story about Nikolaj's re-encounter with the place where he grew up. In the prologue, the 39 year old Nikolaj is driving towards a high school located close to Rykkinn, where he gives a lecture on the idea of society represented by the satellite towns. After the lecture he leaves the school and drives towards Rykkinn. The epilogue begins when he arrives at Rykkinn and visits his old father at an old people's home. During the ride something has happened to Nikolaj. In the prologue he hears a cacophony of noise under the bonnet, the view is fragmentary, and the frozen patterns on the windscreen looks like letters torn apart. In the epilogue the view is better and the noise from the engine has disappeared.

What is important here, is that the story about his childhood and adolescence is framed by an almost continuous story dated 2004, and in this story we find the conditions under which the story of his past is told. To be more precise, in the framing story there is a gap or eclipse, which does not last for long, only those five to ten minutes you need to drive from the high school at Rud to the satellite town in Rykkinn, but it is during this lacuna that the story of his adolescence is told. However, this story is not included in the book in the form of a remembrance or a daydream, as in many autobiographical novels. On the contrary, it is inserted in the form of an epileptic attack. The title of the prologue is "A sudden outburst" ("Et plutselig utbrudd"), which is a translation of the word "epilepsia", and during his lecture at the high school, Nikolaj has a small epileptic attack, and he characterises his relation to his past as the epileptic's relation to himself during the absence. When he drives towards Rykkinn after the lecture, he seems to have an even more serious epileptic attack. More precisely, the account of his youth is told during the absence of the adult Nikolaj, and it is told by an anonymous voice in third person. This textual voice is identical neither with the adult Nikolaj nor with the young Nikolaj, but it is this voice which transforms the autobiographical story into a fictional text. Therefore, *Teori og praksis* is not a fictional novel because it is first and foremost an account of invented events, people and places, but because no one except the voice in the text can sign and take responsibility of the account.

Let's take a closer look at the 15 photographs included in the fictional text. Some of these photographs show different views of Rykkinn; others are more private, like the two portraits of Nikolaj and his friends. There are also photographs referring to the contemporary historical context: the image of the fire on the oil-platform Bravo in 1977, and the advertisement poster for Cuba chocolate. The most striking function of the photographs is that they document the scenes and events depicted in the text. They are markers of authenticity, imprints of something that has happened. The photographs gives the book a documentary function, they certify that Rykkinn is a real place and that Nikolaj was there. Above, I indicated how the text draws the line structurally between autobiography and novel, nonfiction and fiction, by inscribing the account of his childhood in the form of an epileptic attack. There is a similar reversal between reality and fiction at work in the photographs as well. Even if many of the photographic images draw the novel towards the autobiographical and non-fictional, they also reveal that the fictional and the literary are at work in the reality depicted by the text. In several of the pictures one can see letters, writing and graffiti; and in others the images are intertwined with textual descriptions of hallucinations.

On several occasions the book's subject is photography, and the very first is a passage about Nikolaj's elder brother Ivan, who wants to become a photographer. He has taken hundreds of photographs, and we are told that the walls in a basement room are covered with photographs. Nikolaj likes to look at the images because there is always a *surprise* in them, and he is particularly struck by certain details: faces, hands, an eyebrow, a kitchen knife, a care tyre and a strip of asphalt. Later on these photographs are mentioned as copies of things which do not exist any more and on closer examination all the details mentioned are related metonymically to the death of Nikolaj's mother.

At the end of the novel, particularly in the chapter "The photographs", the pictures are no longer placed in a basement, but in the living room, which has a very different metaphorical meaning in the text. Hanging on the wall in the living room they appear as evidence of something which no longer exists in the life of Nikolaj, namely his happy family. At this point in the story, the mother is dead, the widower lays in bed sick with grief, the elder brother has moved, the younger brother lives with an aunt, and Nikolaj is hallucinating on the very edge of madness. After looking at the photographs of the happy family from the past, he leaves the apartment carrying a sleeping bag, a walkman and a Polaroid camera he has inherited from his mother. Then he camps in a forest between a shopping mall and the blocks of flats. There he lays in his sleeping bag, listening to a violin concerto by Mahler recorded on a tape which once belonged to his mother, and shoots photographs of the apartment houses where the driver who killed his mother lives, according to an earlier hallucination in the text.

One night Nikolaj notices that the block of flats has started to move very slowly and the whole satellite town seems to contract. This impression becomes an obsession that is more and more convincing, for him as well as for the reader, since there is no demarcation line in the text between the hallucinations and the reality. Every ten minutes he takes a photograph of the blocks of flat from the very same position, and one of those photographs is reproduced in the book.

ner å ta bilder av Evensen-blokkene bak senteret. Med en følelse av at det er dette han har ventet på, tar han bilder av blokkene. For hvert tiende minutt tar han det samme bildet fra den samme vinkelen. På gressbakken foran KI-senteret legger han bildene utover og leter etter tegn på bevegelse.

Om natten ligger han sammenkrøllet i soveposen, nå fryser han. Regnet fosser omkring ham. Blokkene beveger seg. Han ser for seg farens ansikt ved hageporten.

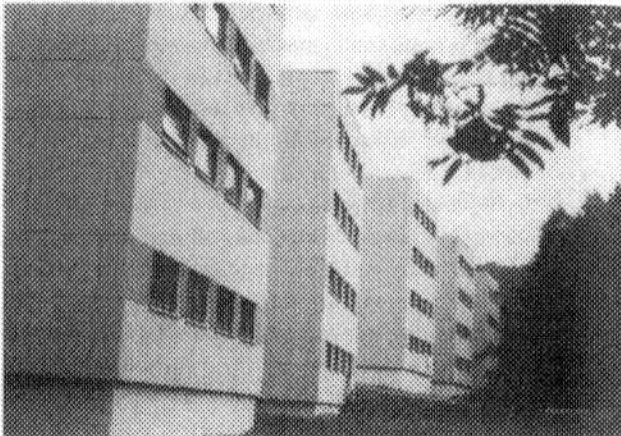

40. «Det beveger seg»

På muren under den skinnende lampen snakker han med en jente som sikkert ikke er mer enn tolv år gammel, likevel er hun så stein på heroin at hun ikke klarer å sitte oppreist. Han må støtte henne der hun sitter foran de stengte inngangsdørene. Det er ingen biler på parkeringsplassen. Ingen Securitas-vakter i bygningen. Sprukket måne på himmelen.

De beveger seg, sier han.

Jenta vipper frem og tilbake på muren.

Blokkene, sier han.

Med smale øyne kikker jenta opp på ham. Nikolaj viser henne fotografiene han har tatt og som med all mulig tydelighet viser at blokkene faktisk har beveget seg noen centimeter det siste døgnet.

Et ørlite jordskjelv, forklarer han.

Utrolig, sier jenta med sovende stemme.

De trekker seg nærmere, sier han.

Ja?

Nikolaj og jenta kikker på bildene sammen.

Senere ligger han under busken igjen. Mahler-kassetten går i stykker, båndet vikler seg rundt fingrene hans og han blir nødt til å kaste den. En bil kjører i sirkel omkring på parkeringsplassen, men han ser ikke hvem som kjører. I blokken bak seg får han øye på en mann i et vindu.

269

Figure 4. Reproduction of page 268–269.

We see five white buildings surrounded by a dark lawn and an even darker forest. Over this, a flat, white sky, and in the front of the image some leaves from a tree. The view is of Rykkinn and depicts the blocks of flats mentioned in the text, but because of the textual description, the photographic perspective and the camera lens, the reader can almost see what the hallucinating Nikolaj saw, and thus repeat his hallucinating gaze. The reader can almost see on the photograph that the blocks of flats are moving, and this experience is confirmed by a twelve year old girl who the hallucinating Nikolaj meets. The scene is this: Nikolaj displays the pictures he has taken, and according to Nikolaj they clearly show that the blocks of flats actually have moved: "A tiny little earthquake, he explains. Incredible, says the girl with a sleepy voice. They contract, he says. Yes? Nikolaj and the girl look at the images together."[24]

The young girl's hesitating approval with the "yes" and the wonderfully placed question mark, both confirm and question Nikolaj's

---

24 "Et ørlite jordskjelv, forklarer han. Utrolig, sier jenta med sovende stemme. De trekker seg sammen, sier han. Ja? Nikolaj og jenta kikker på bildene sammen." (N. Frobenius 2004, 269).

statement. Her "yes" strengthens the coincidence between the textual description and the photographic depiction of the satellite town, while her question mark indicates a difference, a cleavage, between the pictures and the words. This difference is never articulated by the young girl, but only indicated in the text by the question mark. However, the difference between the text and the photographs is re-established when a policeman appears, and resolutely repudiates that the blocks of flats are moving, and prohibits Nikolaj from taking more pictures: "It is over now, says the policeman. You are not going to take any more photos here."[25]

On the level of the story the policeman appears because Nikolaj has become schizophrenic, and has to be admitted to "The Institution of Recuperation of Reality". On the level of a phototextual reading, the appearance of the policemen is motivated by the fact that the novel is about to transform the photographs into mere hallucinations, first by bringing the reader to the point where they almost document the fictional universe established by the text, then by making the young girl see what Nikolaj sees in the photographs, and thus abolishing the distinction between the levels of reality and fiction in the novel's imaginary universe. We, the phototextual readers, can see the photograph from the perspective of the hallucinating Nikolaj, from the perspective of the young girl with the sleepy voice and from the point of view of the resolute policeman, and the photograph is developed differently depending on the perspective we take. The consequence is that the photograph starts to revolve, being a document of the reality of the policeman and the reality of the hallucinating Nikolaj as well as the shifting perspective indicated by the girl. At this point both the text and the photographs float in an ongoing transformation between fiction and reality, hallucination and perception. The hallucinations are no longer components in a realistically described world we can relate them to, but the distinction between fiction and reality is set in motion. Nikolaj's hallucinations are no longer a theme in the text, but the text as well as the photographs has become mad in the sense that the distinction between fiction and reality can't be determined.

---

[25] "Det er over nå, sier politimannen. Du skal ikke fotografere mer her." (N. Frobenius 2004, 270).

Towards a Theory of Phototextuality

I started this presentation of the field of phototextuality by a short history of the term and an introductory definition of the concept phototextuality. I will end this essay by returning to the definition and elaborate it on the background of my research. What appears when we assume the bifocal perspective where the interaction between writing and photography becomes a field of critical investigation? What characterises the relationship between photographs and text in the phototextual tradition? What constitutes the phototextuality of the phototext? Let me propose some reflections and considerations on these questions against the background of my research into the phototextual tradition.

The first element to appear in the phototext is obviously the interaction between the text and the photographic image. When we observe their interaction one aspect which stands out as decisive is the temporal function of the phototext, and the appearance of the temporal difference between the textual narrative and the photographic image. The temporal difference seems to recur in all the books I have considered above. The time that appears on the photographs is always different from the time of the narrative unfolding of the story. For instance, when the hero in *Bruges-la-Morte* leaves his apartment strolling along the canals we are told in the text that it is a grey November afternoon, while the related photograph depicts the canals on a sunny spring day. Examining the temporal relationship between the text and the photographs in the novel, Edwards concludes that the photographs are related to "an indefinable past". A similar temporal difference between the text and the photographs can be traced in Breton's *Nadja*, where the photograph, as Marja Wareheim argues, "records only one moment in the temporal trajectory" of the story, and thus "injects an element of finality into his account."[26] While the written account is open and in a sense unfinished, the photographs are associated with past moments and a sense of loss. Or as Nikolaj terms it in Frobenius' novel *Teori og praksis*, photographs are images of *that which no longer is*. This seminal understanding of the photographic image is theoretically elaborated in Barthes' *Camera Lucida*, where the specificity of the photographic image is defined by

[26] M. Wareheim 1996, 47.

its temporality as an image of something "having-been-there". I will therefore propose that the primary function of phototextuality is the temporal distance separating the photographic image and the written text. The temporal function accentuates the distance between the photograph and the text, and this distance inaugurates a set of phototextual possibilities for interactions and interferences. The temporal distance between the photographs and the text may be reduced to an absolute minimum, as seems to be the case in *The Home Place* by Morris, where the images shows the views of the protagonist, or it may appear as irreducible as in *Bruges-la-Mort* and pushed to the extreme, as is the case in *Camera Lucida*, where the past of photography is placed outside memory – as a past without present. The temporal function of the phototext not only marks the distance between the text and the photograph, but also opens a field of literary and textual possibilities, which can be realised in a series of different forms.

The second aspect to appear in the phototext is the referential or documentary function. Without doubt, the photographs establish a closer relationship to the context than is possible with solely a written text. The importance of the referential function may have been reduced by digital photography, but still photography is a medium with a closer relationship to the referent than language. This seems particularly to be the case in the phototextual tradition I have examined above. From the prefatory note in *Bruges-la-Morte* to *Nadja* and *The Home Place* to *Camera Lucida* and *Teori og praksis* the photographs are described as imprints of pieces of reality, and the use of photographic images is motivated by a certain critique of literary descriptions and the conventional relationship between words and objects. While the link between words and reality is, as Rodenbach points out, arbitrary, the link between photographs and reality is traditionally understood as necessary. This understanding of the specificity of the photographic image is still central in contemporary theories of phototextuality. In the introduction to the anthology *Phototextuality* we can read that "[...] the uniqueness of photographic textuality resides in the unassailably referential nature of the photographic entity."[27] The referential function of the phototext is not only an epistemological or ontological problem, but also important for an understanding of the reading of the phototext. What the reader of the phototext notices is that the text refers to the photographic images. The very presence of photographs strengthens and supplements

[27] A. Huges 2003, 4.

the referential function of the text by presenting to the reader what seems to be a document of the described event.

The third aspect to appear is the series of different and heterogeneous effects of the phototextual interaction. The interaction initiated by the temporal and referential function of language has at least two comprehensible effects. The most common is without doubt that the text attributes new connotations to the photographic image and thereby transforms and structures our understanding of the depicted motif. The first theorist to observe the increasing significance of the photographic image in modern society was Walter Benjamin. In "A Short History of the Photography" he observes that texts and description have a new function in relation to photographs, and claims that the text constitutes a photography that turns all aspects of life into a kind of literature, because it is the text that makes the photographs understandable. In "The Photographic Message" Roland Barthes also notices that texts have become important in relation to photographs, and he designates this relationship as "an important historical reversal".[28]

Often the texts enliven the photographic image with one or more secondary meanings which correspond with what we see on the pictures. This effect of the text is most common outside fictional literature, for instance in journalism, documentary literature like biographies and travelogues, where the main function of the photographs is to document the described reality. This function can be found in the literary phototexts I have examined above as well. For instance in the opening of Frobenius' novel *Teori og praksis* we find an interesting example. The photograph depicts a natural landscape on a sunny day, with a farm, some villas, a forest and fields of grass. Through the text we understand that this is a picture of the place where the satellite town Rykkinn was later constructed, and the text thus transforms the connotation of the photograph by attributing the connotation "the idyllic past" before the establishment of satellite towns in Norway. Nonetheless, the text also attributes other connotations to this particular photograph. In the text the narrator tries to imagine what the place would look like when the satellite town has disappeared in the future. The photograph thus also starts to have connotations with the future this text points towards.

The textual projection of meaning on to the photographic image can also alter our understanding of the referent of the photograph more

[28] R. Barthes 1985, 14.

radically. This seems particularly to be the case when the text contextualises the photographic image, and thus gives a literary description of the reality the photographs depicts. An interesting literary example of this effect is Morris' *The Home Place*, where, as we have seen, the opening paragraph of the book is very close to the first photograph on the opposite page. The words and the image collaborate in the creation of the fictional universe, and this collaboration becomes even more evident later in the story, for instance when the photographs are images of what the fictional protagonist sees when he returns to the place he grew up. A similar interaction between words and images can be found in *Teori og praksis*, particularly in the passages related to the picture of the blocks of flats I discussed above. In these instances the photographs seem to document the imaginary universe constituted primarily by the text, and the text begins to fictionalise the reality imprinted on the photographs. This turning and reversal of the relationship between the photographic referent and the fictional story is without doubt difficult to pinpoint and formalise, but it seems to stand at the very centre of the contemporary explorations of phototextuality.

References

Adams, Timothy Dow 2000, *Light Writing & Life Writing. Photography in Autobiography*. The University of North Carollina Press.

Barthes, Roland 1994, *Camera Lucida. Reflections on Photography*. Transl. Richard Howard, Hill and Wang. A division of Farrar, Strauss and Giroux.

- 1985, "The Photographic Message" in *The Responsibility of Forms: Critical Essays*. Transl. Richard Howard, Basil Blackwell.

- 1980, *La chambre claire. Notes sur la photographie*. Gallimard.

Benjamin, Walter 1980, "A Short History of Phototgraphy" in *Classic Essays on Photography*, Edited by Alan Trachtenberg, Leete's Island Books, New Haven, Connecticut.

- "Kleine Geschichte der Photographie" in *Gessammelte Schriften*, Band II, Suhrkamp Verlag am Main.

Blanchot, Maurice 1993, *The Infinite Conversation*. Transl. Susan Hanson, University of Minnesota Press

- 1969, *L'entretien Infini*. Gallimard.

Breton, André 1999, *Nadja*. Transl. Richard Howard, Penguin Books.

- 1988, *Œuvres Complètes I*, Édition établie par Marguerite Bonnet. Gallimard.

- 1963, Nadja, Gallimard.

Bryant, Marsha 1996, *Photo-Textualities. Reading Photographs and Literature*, Edited by Marsha Bryant, University of Delaware Press, Associated University Press.

Edwards, Paul 2000, "The Photographs in Georges Rodenbach's *Bruges-la-Morte* (1892)" in *European Studies*, Vol. 20, Part 1, p. 71–89.

Frobenius, Nikolaj 2004, *Teori og praksis*. My transl. Gyldendal Norsk Forlag.

Gratton, Johnnie 2003, "Sophie Calle's *Des Histoires Vraies: Irony and Beyond*" in *Phototextualities. Intersections of Phototgraphy and Narrative*, edited by Alex Hughes and Andrea Noble. University of New Mexico Press.

Grojnowski, Daniel 2002, *Photographie et Langage*. José Corti.

Hughes, Alex 2003, *Phototextualities. Intersections of Phototgraphy and Narrative*, edited by Alex Hughes and Andrea Noble. University of New Mexico Press.

Hunter, Jefferson 1987, *Image and Word. The Interaction of Twentieth-Century Photographs and Texts*. Havard University Press.

Morris, Wright 1977, "Photography and Reality. A Conversation between Peter C. Bunnell and Wright Morris" in *Conversations with Wright Morris. Critical Views and Responses*. University of Nebraska Press, Lincoln and London.

- 1948, *The Home Place*. University of Nebraska Press.

Rabb, Jane M. 1995, "Notes Toward a History of Literature and Photography" in *Literature & Photography. Interactionas 1840–1990, A Critical Anthology edited by Jane M. Rabb*. University of New Mexico Press.

Rodenbach, Georges 2005, *Bruges-la-Morte*. Transl. Mike Mitchell and Will Stone, Dedalus.

- 1998, *Bruges-la-Morte*, Presentation par Jean-Pierre Bertrand et Daniel Grojnowski. GF Flammarion.

Valéry, Paul 1980, "The Centenary of Photography" in *Classic Essays on Photography*, Edited by Alan Trachtenberg, Leete's Island Books.

Wareheim, Marja 1996, "Time, and the Surrealist Sensibility" in M. Bryant 1996.

Arne Melberg

Prose

PROSE. Plus facile à faire que les vers.
Flaubert: *Dictionnaire des idées reçues.*

Just as some people work because they're bored, I sometimes write because I have nothing to say. My writing is just like the reverie in which someone avoiding thought would naturally immerse himself with the difference that I am able to dream in prose.
Fernando Pessoa/ Bernardo Soares: *The Book of Disquiet 170.*

In this presentation I will give some glimpses of *prose*: prose regarded as a phenomenon of vast importance in the aesthetical landscape of modernity. Prose is, of course, particularly important in literature but prose as a trend – *prosification* – is affiliated with the trend that is a common denominator to all the contributions to this book: *aestheticisation*. I will discuss some efforts to define or at least delimit prose as a literary, aesthetical and philosophical phenomenon and I will conclude with two literary examples: one on poetry as prose (Harryette Mullen) and one on prose as the challenge to prosaic reality (W.G. Sebald).

Prose: the received idea

Whenever a literary critic or philosopher ponders the meaning of "literature" he turns to poetry: in poetry he finds the "poeticity" and the "literarity" that is meant to be specific to the literary language and therefore the very object of knowledge for the literary critic. Such delimitations belong to modernity: in the classical period literature was instead regarded as *mimetical* and poetry was only one of many options when it came to the literary "imitation" of reality, nature, the ideal or the norm. It may be regarded as a historical irony that poetry was elevated into being literature itself at the very moment when the most important literary expressions were no longer poetry, but rather novels or fiction. Or perhaps *prose*. The modernisation of poetry and its liberation from classical forms of poetic expression has meant that poetry has converged with prose. And the most prominent efforts to define literature in terms of "literarity" and "poeticity" were actually made in exactly the period when poetry was approaching prose, i.e. during the first half of the 20th Century.

But what, then, is *prose*? Considering the dominance of prose in modern literature it is somewhat surprising that literary theory is reticent when it comes to discussing the meaning of prose: I have at least not found any massive effort – comparable to the efforts to define poetry – to define prose as a phenomenon, as a historical fact or as a tendency. In the words of Roland Greene and Elizabeth Fowler: "Like a kind of Antarctica, prose remains one of the last undefined, untheorized bodies of writing in early modern European languages"[1] – a comment that aims at the Renaissance but is in my view quite as pertinent in modern times. There are, of course, great efforts to delimit the character of *narrative prose*, starting with Shklovsky's *Theory of Prose* (1929) through to Todorov's *Poetics of Prose* (1971), and perhaps one could regard all that "narratology" that has emanated from the works of Gérard Genette, precisely as efforts to determine the qualities of narrative, fictional prose. But when I am considering the possibility of modern literature and modern culture being invaded by prose, then I am not only thinking of narrative fiction. Fiction is of course an important member of the literary family of prose but still only one of many members in a family that also includes quite a lot of that which is vaguely called the literature of fact.[2] Yes, the very effort to draw a stable line between fictional and factual prose, an effort that can be traced to Shklovsky, is an important contribution to the *doxa* of prose: the notion that prose is *either* fictional and therefore literary *or* factual and therefore not literary – a notion that seems vaguely connected to another and probably more basic notion: that poetry is opposed to prose.

So: what is prose? I will start sketching an answer by discussing some theoretical aspects of prose and I will start with the *doxa* of

---

1 Greene & Fowler 1997, p. 1.

2 Shklovsky ends his *Theory of Prose* with a short chapter on "Essay and Anecdote," where he discusses "plotless prose" while reserving the fictional plot as characteristic for "high literature." And Shklovsky already wants to reverse the prominent tendency that I am aiming at here: "The development of a literature of fact should not attempt to emulate high literature but rather to part company with it." (Shklovsky 1990, p. 209).

prose: the explicit or implicit notions of what prose is (and is not), notions that have become part of our cultural unconscious and function unquestioned when it comes to our designations of "literature"; notions that guide those institutional reflexes used in our classification and evaluation of literature in for instance libraries, book-stores, literary critique, analysis, teaching.

The most important components of this *doxa* seem to be the following: prose being regarded as the natural state of language; literary prose regarded as fictional prose; fictional prose regarded as something that connects what otherwise would stay unconnected in a meaningful *plot*.

My critique of this *doxa* does not mean that I regard every component as erroneous but that the overall picture tends to be misleading due to its being structured according to principles that I call *metaphysical*; and the impact of metaphysics is to lock our thinking in absolute opposites, in either-or juxtapositions. And in this case we meet a whole series of opposites that may be internally incongruent but still add up to the metaphysical *doxa* of prose: language is *either* natural, fluent, unreflected, communicative *or* it is literary and resists communication. Literary language is *either* poetry *or* prose. Prose is *either* literary (and then it is fiction) *or* not literary (and deals with the facts of reality). The metaphysics of language and literature invites us to think according to the pattern already made parodical by Molière in these words of the simplistic Monsieur Jourdain: "Everything that is prose is not verse; and everything that is not verse is prose."[3] (And here is another metaphysical mistake in disguise: "verse" as equivalent with "poetry").

"The first point to get clear about prose is that the language of ordinary speech is not prose, or at least prose only to the extent that it is not verse." This is a quote from the heading "Verse and prose" in *Princeton Encyclopedia of Poetry and Poetics*. That goes against one misunderstanding – prose being (like) spoken language – while installing another: prose and poetry ("verse") being absolutely contrary. Let me stick to the first part: neither poetry nor prose is a natural form of language. Prose, like poetry, is a written version of language and prose as well as poetry can be used for a literary and rhetorical cultivation of language. Roland Barthes asks himself what

[3] "Tout ce qui est prose n'est point vers; et tout ce qui n'est point vers est prose." *Le Bourgeois Gentilhomme* III:3.

transforms a linguistic utterance into art and answers: *rhetoric*. "It is this specific element which, for my part, I shall call *rhetoric*, so as to avoid any restriction of poetics to poetry and in order to mark our concern with a general level of language common to all genres, *prose and verse alike*."[4] Rhetoric excludes the notion of a linguistic natural state and installs discursive thinking. The result is that the opposition prose-poetry breaks down into a series of rhetorical and/ or literary devices and strategies that sometimes make poetry and prose go in different directions; but can sometimes make them get involved or even coincide.

Doxa: that is the culturally unconscious. Consciousness about prose makes you realise that it is not a natural state and that it cannot be equated with spoken language. Those who have examined prose historically tend to mean that it is "a late and sophisticated development in the history of literature" – I am again quoting from the article in *Princeton Encyclopedia* mentioned above. Efforts have been made to localise the emergence of prose to medieval liturgical habits, where verse means change and break while prose means continuity and sequence, for example by extending the final vowel in a *Halleluja* and making it introduce the following sequence. I have borrowed this example from Henri Meschonnic, who includes a chapter on the relation between poetry and prose in his monumental work *Critique du rythme* (1982), where he develops a fundamental critique of the opposition of poetry to prose. Meschonnic: "Prose, poetry: all theoretical and political problems of writing including its historicity are involved in this opposition."[5] The problems have to do with prose as well as poetry being misunderstood and devaluated: prose taken as a neutral and natural state (poetry as art and artifice), prose as dialogical (poetry as monological), prose as transparent communication (poetry as opaque and self-referential) etc. Forgetting that poetry as well as prose consists of discursive forms you risk missing the effects of interaction and interference that emerge when poetry and prose share their means of expression. Meschonnic again: "Prose has never stopped entering verse, and verse entering prose. Other forms than those of Western modernity did not even know of this opposition."[6]

---

4 Barthes 1986, p. 83. My italics.

5 "Prose, poésie: tous les problèmes théoriques et politiques de l'écriture, son historicité, sont en jeu dans cette opposition." Meschonnic 1982, p. 395.

6 "La prose n'a cessé d'entrer dans le vers, le vers, d'aller à la prose. D'autres formes que celles de la modernité occidentale n'ont même pas connu cette opposition." Ib. p. 457.

And I want to add: if the *doxa* of modern literature tends to take poetry and prose in different directions, then there is also a tendency of *prosification*. Today, more than ever, traditional literary forms of expression are submitted to this tendency that is also operative in bringing different art forms into a closer cooperation (a tendency I will come back to).

Prosification

In the literary field we can recognise the tendency that I call *prosification* in all those new constellations that were developed during the 20th Century and, not least, today. I am considering conflicting trends here: on the one hand those institutional efforts to keep genres and forms apart according to the literary metaphysics sketched above; on the other hand the ongoing efforts to cross boundaries provoked by both writers and readers and resulting in those expressive forms that from an institutional point of view are "mixed" or "hybrid" forms. Let me summarise *prosification* in two such mixtures – poetry/prose, fiction/fact – and then add a glimpse of the art forms during modernism and post-modernism.

Poetry/prose

In a series of essays from the 1920s and onwards Roman Jakobson tried to determine the "poetical" and "prosaic" extremes of language, arriving at the conclusion that poetry aims to a metaphorical extreme while prose works metonymically. Thus Jakobson contributed to the ontology of poetry that has been a striking feature of the literary theory that was inspired by high modernism, and defining the essence of literature as "poeticity" – while tending to forget that Jakobson insisted on the *interrelation* between poetry and prose. According to Jakobson, neither metaphorical poetry nor metonymical prose can stay pure, but they are interrelated – and it is the tendency of these interrelations that I like to call *prosification*. Even such an important contributor to the poetics of high modernism as the French poet Paul Claudel had an eye for the prosaic tendency to judge from this statement from 1925: "And after all, poetry and prose have today come to a stage in their development where they would gain by marrying their resources."[7] It is this tense "marriage" that Jakobson tries to describe through the interrelations between the metaphorical and the metonymical tendencies; and a "marriage" between poetry and prose was already celebrated with those "prose poems" that Baudelaire mostly published in newspapers and journals and that were collected after his death as *Petits poèmes en prose* (1869). Baudelaire was read by an admiring Nietzsche, who devoted section 92 in *The Gay Science* to the relation between *Prose and Poetry*. Nietzsche writes:

> Consider, that the great masters of prose almost always had been poets … and truly, you can only write good prose *facing poetry*! Because prose is an ongoing nice little war with poetry: all its charm consists in poetry being permanently evaded and contradicted. /---/ and there are thousands of pleasures in this war, including losses, and unpoetical people, so-called prose-people, know nothing about that: – because these people write and talk only bad prose! *War is the father of all good things*, war is also the father of good prose.[8]

Nietzsche has his Greeks in mind, as always, and what he calls "war" is the Greek *polemos*, and that could just as well be rendered as polemics, interaction or interchange. Nietzsche's brilliant intuition anticipates the development of modern poetry as an ongoing interaction between poetry and prose, an interaction that can take very many forms. But they all have in common an opposition against that cultivation of poetical expression as negation – negation of prose, of colloquial language, of communication – characteristic for the high modernist poetry that can be traced back to Mallarmé. Nietzsche's "war" can actually be associated with Jakobson's tense "marriage" between metaphor and metonymy and beyond to the settlement with high modernism that Paul Celan articulated in his so called Meridian-talk (1960). Here Celan identifies the tradition of modern poetry with

---

[7] "Et cependent, la poésie et la prose sont arrivées aujourd'hui à un point de dévelopment où elles gagnerait à marier leurs ressources." Quoted from Meschonnic 1982, p. 501.

[8] "Man beachte doch, dass die grossen Meister der Prosa fast immer Dichter gewesen sind … und fürwahr, man schreibt nur *im Angesichte der Poesie* gute Prosa! Denn diese ist ein ununterbrochener artiger Krieg mit der Poesie: alle ihre Reize bestehen darin, dass beständig der Poesie ausgewichen und widersprochen wird. /---/ und so giebt es tausend Vergnügungen des Krieges, die Niederlagen mitgezählt, von denen die unpoetischen, die sogenannten Prosa-Menschen, gar nichts wissen: - diese schreiben und sprechen denn auch nur schlechte Prosa! *Der Krieg ist der Vater aller guten Dinge*, der Krieg ist auch der Vater guten Prosa." Nietzsche 1988, p. 447f. My translation.

"Mallarmé" and he tries to think "Mallarmé consequently to the end." At the far end of Mallarmé and high modernism Celan finds neither the autonomy of poetry not its isolation or the negation of language; instead he finds a *meeting*. Even the most lonely of all poems is situated in "*the secret of the meeting.*"[9] The meeting: that is the peaceful and one might say existential version of the "war" that Nietzsche already pointed out. Meeting, war, marriage, interaction, interchange: thus we can understand the development of modern poetry in its relation to prose and against prose, a development I name *prosification*.

Fiction/fact

According to a stubborn component of our literary *doxa*, fictional prose is real literature, while factual prose is dismissed as non-literary, simply communicative and transparently referring to a more real reality. This is misguided for several reasons: partly because many versions of factual prose use literary means in order to create credibility when giving words to the facts of reality. Truth is not (or not only) a question of the referential correspondence between words and reality. Linguistic truth has to be produced, meaning simply that even those representations of reality that are non fictional and aim for simple truth also use literary devices. The examples are most striking in the vast literary area in the borderline of what is conventionally regarded as real literature, i.e. essay and biography and new-journalism and all versions of "documentary" literature, but can also be seen in the most sober and factual prose.

Fiction – a phenomenon that is about as loosely historicised and defined as "prose" – actually only operates within a small part of the literary field. Furthermore, fiction does not always want to stay within the limits of fiction . In the history of the novel, new fictions are permanently invented but fiction is just as often revoked and overruled. In contemporary novelistic literature one observes an urge for reality that does not stop within the traditional limits of fiction. Literary prose could mean fiction but prose could also confine itself to using elements of fiction or even resist fiction without leaving its literary character behind. According to Peter Bürger's analysis

---

9 "Mallarmé konsequent zu Ende denken." "Im Geheimnis der Begegnung." Celan 1988, p. 48, 55.

of what he calls the prose of modernity, *Prosa der Moderne* (1988), narrative fiction has become an almost insurmountable task for the modern writer, since the experience to be represented, the prominent characteristic of modernity, is *Kontingenz*: the modern novel deals with contingency, "contingency, however, cannot be narrated."[10] This statement seems to me to be strongly exaggerated; still, I am tempted to use *prose* as an umbrella-term for the collected efforts – fictive, non-fictive, quasi-fictive – to express and handle the contingency of modernity. Prose: the term that describes the approach of fiction to reality and the ways that factual writing describes reality.

A glimpse of the arts during modernity

The prose poem of the 19th Century opened the way for the prosification of literature in the 20th Century; and there is an analogous tendency in a musical phenomenon that emerges in the second half of the 19th Century called *musical prose*. The term described the efforts to break down the long musical and melodic periods of the symphony in favour of a descriptive and painterly expression, loosen operatic conventions in order to approach a dramatic dialogue with *Sprechgesang*.[11] The term was picked up by Arnold Schönberg in order to describe his examination of an "atonality", where all components (all twelve elements of the scale chosen) were equally important and their interrelation meant everything. Musical prose in Schönberg's version was a great effort to handle (and fight) musical contingency and transform music into a significant language close to prose. And Schönberg regarded prose according to the principle that Friedrich Schlegel articulated in one of his fragments: "in true prose everything must be underlined."[12]

Schönberg's non-melodic musical prose was developed at the same time as non-figurative art was developed by the cubists (Bracque, Picasso), based on the efforts of Cézanne to present nature and things in their formation. The result was a construction of relations, surfaces and connections where nobody had seen connections before; again an endeavour to handle the contingency of modern reality. Only a couple of years later Marcel Duchamp presented prosaic everyday

[10] Bürger 1988, p. 391.
[11] See Carl Dahlhaus 1982, p. 154ff.
[12] "In der wahren Prosa müsse alles unterstrichen sein." *Athenäumsfragment* 395.

tools and things as works of art; and in the 1920s the works of art were infiltrated by the prose of reality by way of collage and montage. There is a seemingly straight line from these avant-garde beginnings to the performative versions of music and art that were developed in the 1950s and 1960s by John Cage and Joseph Beuys – and further on into the contemporary post-modern scene of art.

There are of course obvious medial and technological and other differences between visual art, music and literature – and there is an impressive effort in modernist theory to keep them ontologically apart – but there are also striking coincidences. What they have in common is a tendency that might be called *aestheticisation*: new things, areas and activities are included in an aesthetical concept and given aesthetical function. These areas are often every-day and these things are prosaic, meaning that the aesthetical practice that emerges not only gives life to art but also aims to transform life into art. And that should mean that the tendency of aestheticisation is also a prosification (and prosification an aestheticisation): strategies for handling the contingencies of modern life.

The philosophy of prose

Literary prose may be a "late" and "sophisticated" invention – according to the article from *Princeton Encyclopedia* quoted above – but I nevertheless have an impression that its literary character is quickly neutralised or normalised: prose is regarded as the standard state of language. A sophisticated version of such a normalisation is analysed by Jeffrey Kittay & Wlad Godzich in *The Emergence of Prose* (1987), where they examine the history of prose maintaining that prose is easily situated as a "background": "Prose can situate itself in a foundational position with respect to all language. It will under-stand and under-write speech and verse. But it will not display such understanding, which would only bring it out of the background that is its ground."[13] I am sceptical to the ontological fundamentalism that Kittay & Godzich are flirting with here – prose as the foundation of language – but they nevertheless point to an interesting characteristic: the *discretion* of prose, its artifice when it comes to appearing as non-artificial. And I believe that this characteristic cooperates with the liturgical capacity

13 Kittay & Godzich 1987, p. 198.

pointed out by Meschonnic (and many others): the prosaic joining together of what would otherwise be separate and thereby creating continuity and coherence. That is: the capacity of prose to handle contingency. These two formal characteristics – prose appearing as non-art(ificial) and prose creating continuity – can be combined into a conceptual framework that I would like to call *the philosophy of prose*, and that I want to touch on with the help of Walter Benjamin. I am considering now a fragment written, according to Benjamin's editor, around the time of his last completed work from 1940, *On the Concept of History* (*Über den Begriff der Geschichte*), and called "The dialectical image" ("Das dialektische Bild"). I have translated the relevant parts:

> If you want to regard history as a text, then you have to do what a later writer said about the literary text: the past has located pictures in this text, which could be compared to a plate that is sensitive to light. /---/ The historical method is a philology, that is based upon the book of life. 'To read what was never written', according to Hofmannsthal. The reader we are talking about is the true historian.
>
> The plurality of histories reminds us of the plurality of languages. Universal history in the modern sense could only be a kind of esperanto. The idea of a universal history is a messianic one. /---/ Its language is integral prose, that has burst the fetters of writing and will be understood by all people (like the language of birds by Sunday children). – The idea of prose coincides with the messianic idea of universal history (the versions of literary prose as the spectrum of the universally historian /---/).[14]

In this fragment Benjamin speculates on the "text" of History as the book of life that will never be read to its end and on the language of "universal history" as "prose". Already in his much earlier work on the concept of "critique" in German Romanticism he had examined the idea of "absolute" prose as an accomplishment of the arts and of poetry: prose is there called "the idea of poetry" and "the

[14] "Will man die Geschichte als einen Text betrachten, dann gilt von ihr, was ein neuerer Autor von literarischen sagt: die Vergangenheit habe in ihnen Bilder niedergelegt, die man denen vergleichen könne, die von einer lichtempfindlichen Platte festgehalten werden. /---/ Die historische Methode ist eine philologische, der das Buch des Lebens zugrunde liegt. 'Was nie geschrieben wurde, lesen', heißt es bei Hofmannsthal. Der Leser, an den hier zu denken ist, ist der wahre Historiker.

Die vielheit der Historien ist der Vielheit der Sprachen ähnlich. Universalgeschichte im heutigen Sinn kann immer nur eine Art von Esperanto sein. Die Idee der Universalgeschichte ist eine messianische. /---/ Seine Sprache ist integrale Prosa, die die Fesseln der Schrift gesprengt hat und von allen Menschen verstanden wird (wie die Sprache der Vögel von Sonntagskindern). – Die Idee der Prosa fällt mit der messianischen Idee der Universalgeschichte zusammen (die Arten der Kunstprosa als das Spektrum der universalhistorischen /---/). Benjamin 1991 I:3, p. 1238. My translation.

notion of the idea of poetry as prose determines the whole of romantic aesthetic philosophy" as a "basic thought" with an "effect" that is still to come.[15] On this stage of his meditation on "prose" Benjamin is inspired by Novalis and Friedrich Schlegel; at the time of the fragment quoted above he had developed an idea of "universal history" and his "prose" now has a "messianic" perspective: only when "everything" exists in an unanimous "now" (*allseitiger und integraler Aktualität*) could one talk about an accomplished "universal history." In the history where we live "universal history" is a mere possibility or a dimension that can be glimpsed in our linguistic and cultural multiplicity or perhaps find an expression in artificial ways ("esperanto"). In a utopian perspective, however, "universal history" can be expressed and understood by everyone in a unanimous language, a language Benjamin calls "prose". He writes *integrale Prosa* just as he writes *integraler Aktualität* about the messianic moment; the adjective emphasises the fact that prose is producing simultaneity and concurrence. In Benjamin's "universal history" *everything* is connected; but since it is impossible to reach this destination in real history one could just as well say that our world, here and now, is ruled by contingency: *everything* is temporary and accidental and lacks definite meaning.

What I regard as a philosophy of prose is not only Benjamin's far-fetched ideas about ideal "prose" but most of all his effort to find connections and create meaning – finding the hidden (or possible) relations in the fragmentary, broken and contingent reality of modernity. In his fragment Benjamin relates himself to a powerful tradition of thought that goes back at least to German Romanticism. As early as Hegel, this figure of thought had been established as a commonplace. Hegel, in his lectures on aesthetics from around 1830, discusses the literary prose that he met in the modern novel as corresponding to "the prose of reality."[16] Prose, regarded as the fundamental condition of modern life and the very structure of modern reality, is actually of as great importance in Hegel's aesthetical thinking as it is for the development of the novel. There is a distinct line of thought here from for instance Flaubert, who tried to find adequate expression for prosaic reality, to the catchy title given by the philosopher Maurice Merleau-Ponty to one of his works from the 1950s: *La prose du monde*.

---

[15] Benjamin 1991 I:1, p. 101.

[16] "Prosa der Wirklichkeit". Hegel 1970, p. 219.

The view of the world and its reality as prosaic hides an idea of poetry as an indication of a very different reality. According to Hegel this poetry had finally lost its possibilities in the prose of bourgeois society – Hegel predicts the "end of the epoch of art" – but that does not stop the idea from a more or less eternal return: as poetry, art, dream, utopia, fantasy. The idea of poetry as a contrast to prose is strikingly put by Emily Dickinson in poem 657, where she describes her poetical life as a kingdom of possibilities in comparison to being shut up in prose:

> I dwell in Possibility –
> A fairer House than Prose –
> More numerous of Windows –
> Superior – for Doors –

And in poem 613 she describes the meaning of prose as closure and stagnation (and that is of course the flip side of prose as a creator of connections and continuity):

> They shut me up in Prose –
> As when a little Girl
> They put me in the Closet –
> Because they liked me "still" –

There are of course leaps of thought between Hegel, Dickinson, Benjamin and Merleau-Ponty. The commonplace that Dickinson varies so nicely – prose as the necessity of reality – Benjamin seems to turn on its head by imagining utopian prose as a tool for a "universal history", transformed in a "messianic" moment making all different languages into one. There is, however, a connection here that I believe goes back to the liturgical origin of prose: joining together. Dickinson's prose is a mechanism of closure. Benjamin's prose finds new connections, makes a whole out of fragments and integrates what is disintegrated. The patterns of thought are affiliated and they stretch to what I described above as the handling of contingency in modern art. For the philosophers of prose the task is to find or invent connections that give meaning to the contingency of existence; and the task is to transform the necessities of already existing connections into possibilities.

The poetry of prose: Harryette Mullen

The modernisation of poetry during the 20th Century can be described as a prosification: traditional poetical signals, depending on metrics, rhythm, rhyme, became less important and opened a space for new ways of triggering language with poetical function. Several new strategies were due to the fact that poetry (at least Western poetry) was no longer considered as an oral performance but was written on paper for a book-page; meaning that effects of repetition and scanning gave way to visual arrangements. While this historical change was going on it may have been perceived as if "natural" forms were substituted by artificial forms; and in this sense the modern development of poetry runs parallel with the development mentioned above in musical art from melody into the "musical prose" of serial music; in visual art from figurality into abstract colour and form and in contemporary art: performance and concept. There seems, however, to be a unanimous view of the modernisation of poetry as a work of language, as an increased attention to the linguistic expression – and such is also the bearing of Roman Jakobson's various definitions of the poetical function. This view of poetry approaches an ontological determination: poetry is considered an autonomous linguistic expression that can be delimited and defined according to its own internal logic.

When I call this well-known logic "prosification" it is an effort to cool down the ontological ambitions and adjust the perspective, thus making us regard the development of poetry in relation to the development of prose. And the characteristic of the organisation of prose, in comparison to poetry, is simply that prose joins together what poetry tends to break up. Prose aims at a continuity that could be understood as meaningful in relation to what I have repeatedly called contingency. The famous poetical attention to linguistic expression is, in such a perspective, not an essential characteristic of poetry: it is rather a strategy. Or, better: it is a bundle of strategies that can all be regarded in relation to prose; strategies aiming at everything between opposition and peaceful cohabitation with a dominant prose (and prose, in its turn, is of course only a general tendency covering an array of linguistic strategies).

The modern prose poem, initiated by Baudelaire, gives a map of such strategies. Baudelaire's prose poem inserts prose into a poetical expression and a poetical view of reality: the prose poem profanes classical poetical motives by taking them "down" to the bizarre level, that is determined by the contingency of modern reality. The prosification strikes not only against traditional forms, expressed in rhyme and rhythm, but also against traditional motives and not least against the subject, that was supposed to be the fountain-head at least of romantic poetry. The prose poems dethrone and dehumanise the traditional subject while giving attention to the impersonal, to materiality and to things. The prose poem in the Baudelarian tradition is not "poetry" but, rather, an examination of what Nietzsche called the "war" between poetry and prose, according to the passage from *The Gay Science* quoted above; an examination of what is prosaic in poetry and what may be poetic in prose.

My example on such an "examination" in a prose poem is taken from the Afro-American writer Harryette Mullen, a page from *Sleeping with the Dictionary* (2002):

> Elliptical
>
> They just can't seem to ... They should try harder to ... They ought to be more ... We all wish they weren't so ... They never ... They always . Sometimes they ... Once in a while they ... However it is obvious that they ... Their overall tendency has been ... The consequences of which have been ... They don't appear to understand that ... If only they would make an effort to ... But we know how difficult it is for them to ... Many of them remain unaware of ... Some who should know better simply refuse to ... Of course, their perspective has been limited by ... On the other hand, they obviously feel entitled to ... Certainly we can't forget that they ... Nor can it be denied that they ... We know that this has had an enormous impact on their ... Nevertheless their behaviour strikes us as ... Our interactions unfortunately have been ...

The title "Elliptical" could refer to the many incomplete sentences that are piled up here in order to form a kind of a "poem". The sentences – or the fragments of sentences – are separated by the three dots that in themselves make up a series of ellipses. The dots are a graphic arrangement that can hardly be imagined in an orally conceived poem unless as pauses and silences. The sentences (or fragments) are separated but also connected by the three dots, that therefore can be seen as a gesture of prose: the dots signal contingency but they still make connections alluding to a lost or never found coherence.

The sentences that are separated (but still connected) by the three dots seem to be lifted out of a kind of meeting, emanating from several voices discussing something together. They seem to discuss for instance a drop-out case or a football team or a research group. It probably does not matter very much what kind of phenomenon they are discussing: the interesting feature is that a discussion is going on and that the poem gives a fragmentary account of this. We can sense a development in the discussion: the fragments express disappointment, and in spite of some lines that look like understanding objections, the final ellipse probably states that the discussion will end in an unfavourable conclusion for the person or object or association under discussion.

The poem seems therefore to represent a most prosaic situation, for instance taken from the meeting room of the social welfare office. And the meeting discusses a very prosaic reality, for instance the negative behaviour of a client. The conclusion (if there will be a conclusion) will surely be just as prosaic. We have to guess, however, as to the contents of the discussion and the conclusion can only be inferred in an extension of the poem. The poem states nothing. Instead, the poem deals with the voices, or perhaps the sentences, as they are rendered in ellipses and fragments. These sentences are in several ways marked by contingency: we get the impression the choice of voices is made at random and that the beginning is just as arbitrary as the end. The voices and the sentences could just as well keep going (although the poem has had its say). The voices are, furthermore, demonstratively anti-poetical: they express themselves trivially and prosaically about a trivial and prosaic situation. And there is no poetical subject to be found, that can grant us with meaning or even expression.

One could of course discuss if this should be called a poem. Perhaps we should instead regard it as a poetical intervention? Poetry breaks in into this prosaic chatter by interrupting the sentences and arranging the fragments in a pattern with rhythmical qualities, thereby transforming the elliptical sentences into something close to breath. The absent poet listens on our behalf and arranges what she hears in a way that will help us to notice the cruelly prosaic character of the situation – as well as its poetical possibilities. Even the most prosaic language is always on the verge of poetry.

The prose of prose: W. G. Sebald

"My medium is prose, not the novel." Thus W. G. Sebald in an interview from 1993,[17] i.e. several years before he started with *Austerlitz*, that was to be his last book and the only book the he (or the publisher) called a "novel". I suppose that he wanted to signal a distance to fiction and with the concept of "prose" pave the way for the mixture

[17] Sebald 2003, p. 263. All translations from Sebald are mine.

of biography, criticism, documentary, history but also fiction, that make up the sum of his writings.

Sebald left his native Germany early and lived in England as a university teacher. His writings were concluded with *Austerlitz* (2001) while the books preceding this "novel" avoid fictional signals. *The Rings of Saturn* (*Die Ringe des Saturn*, 1995) is subtitled "An English Pilgrimage" and has a walk in Suffolk as a presupposition and frame. But the walk is also a mental journey, in about the same way as it once was for Rousseau in *Les rêveries d'un promeneur solitaire*: wandering in the English landscape leads to a cultural walk in space and time between seemingly completely disparate stations, like for instance examinations of the diseases of elms, the rise and fall of the fishing of herring, glimpses of the 17th Century melancholic Thomas Browne, of Chateaubriand in England, of the timorous Swinburne and the eccentric Edward Fitzgerald, the translator of Omar Khayyam, of the history of imperialism in Congo and in China, of sericulture and of military installations. The narrator is identified as the writer and documented photographically: the text is interfoliated by a number of black-and-white photos, functioning as visual commentaries, including a ten year old picture of the writer, "still ignorant about the unpleasantness that was to come."[18]

Sebald had started involving pictures in his texts already with the earlier books *Vertigo* (*Schwindel. Gefühle*, 1990) and *The Emigrants* (*Die Ausgewanderten,* 1992). An example from the last story in *The Emigrants* illustrates his technique: Sebald tells us about his leaving Germany as a young man and arriving in England, in Manchester, where he becomes acquainted with the painter Max Aurach. The perspective of the narrative gradually shifts to Aurach, who made an earlier escape from Germany and therefore appears as the precursor to the narrator. We are told a lot about Aurach's studio and we are shown a photo of one of his pictures – and that is strikingly reminiscent of a portrait made by the real painter Frank Auerbach, who also had a German past and a famous studio, although not in Manchester but in London. That is how Sebald works: he contracts Auerbach into Aurach and displaces and defers his biography; he works with identification but also by condensating and deferring, i.e. he works with

[18] Sebald 2003 (1995), p. 313: "in Unkenntnis noch der unguten Dinge, die seither geschehen sind."

the mechanisms of a dream. And he adds a deferred signature to his creation by giving his own pet-name Max to his Aurach.

In *Austerlitz* the narrator is subdued or perhaps doubled into a fictional character, Jacques Austerlitz. Or is it perhaps a real person? Sebald gives his Austerlitz an extensive biography that could not be called private or even fictitious since it answers at every point to recent European history. More than that: like in *The Emigrants* and *The Rings of Saturn* the text is interfoliated by a number of black-and-white photos. The fiction – if fiction is the word – is that Austerlitz is an interested photographer keen on documenting his visual impressions, meaning that the extensive discussion concerning modern architecture in railway stations, fortifications, state departments, libraries and prison camps is given photographic support. Furthermore, Austerlitz himself is documented: we see a photo of the bookshelves of his study in London, some pictures of himself as a boy, one turning up when he finds his mother's friend still alive in Prague: "Yes, and this, on the other photo, said Vera after a while, this is you, Jacquot, in the month of February 1939."[19] The photo, also used on the cover of the novel, shows a little boy theatrically dressed up as a page, standing in an anonymous meadow. "I felt", says Austerlitz to the narrator, "pierced by the searching glance from this page, who had come back for his rights."[20]

The situation – that we are given photos of the fictitious title character – is unusual or perhaps even unique when it comes to novels. A photo, accompanied by the words "that is you", is after all something else than a description or an illustration, it is rather a documentation, a statement by a witness (although Sebald characteristically complicates the matter by letting his title character feel "pierced" by the picture although he is not able to recognise himself).

In the earlier books, Sebald as narrator took some responsibility for the photos but he also identifies with the persons he meets or narrates about. In *Austerlitz* we have an anonymous and discreet narrator, who slides from the first to the third person in order to subordinate to his title character, Jacques Austerlitz, who is normally the narrative voice. The porous relationship between narrator and character is emphasised by the way in which Austerlitz is allowed to express himself:

---

[19] Sebald 2003 (2001), p. 266: "Ja, und das hier, auf der anderen Photographie, sagte Vera nach einer Weile, das bist du, Jacquot, im Monat Feber 1939" etc.

[20] Ib. p. 268: "Und immer fühlte ich mich dabei durchdrungen von dem forschenden Blick des Pagen der gekommen war, sein Teil zurückzufordern" etc.

it is often within the narration of the narrator, giving us a prose on many levels like "said x, said y, said z" – a technique that Sebald had learned from working with Thomas Bernhard's meandering prose. As in *The Rings of Saturn*, one could call it a prose that wanders and roves through European history. It is a novel that is also a critical discussion of political, architectural and cultural European history, and it is also a biography. It is a more or less fictitious biography of Jacques Austerlitz, such as he gradually and fragmentarily reconstructs it in his different meetings with the narrator, extended over 30 years and always in different places in Antwerp, London, Paris. Austerlitz, we read, has been transported as a war child from Prague to England, and grown up in a sombre pietistic setting in Wales, before coming to Oxford and London. And only then starting his search for his lost parents, leading him to Prague and again to Paris. It is certainly no continuous wandering or a travel reaching its destination: when the novel ends Austerlitz has only just started his research on the founding history of Europe and himself. Identity, we understand, is a fragmented and changing matter demanding a work without end in order to get started. And that goes for personal identity as well as European identity. The novelistic-prosaic research is precisely such a work.

The whole text is more than 400 pages in one single sequence, without any chapters or even new paragraphs; this is a way of keeping the biographical, historical and critical strands together in one single piece of prose. I have noted altogether three asterisks and a couple of dashes marking pauses and time intervals in the text. The sentences are often long and winding. One is close to ten pages long and piles up information on Terezín (Theresienstadt), where Jacques Austerlitz, who is searching for his own history, has found traces of his mother. But this overwhelming sentence is interfoliated by a couple of photos: one covers a whole page documenting a sociological presentation of 52 different work activities in the camp; another shows a stamp from Theresienstadt indicating an idyllic setting. That is to say that the photos of the novel give us breaks in the otherwise compact prose, at the same time as they are spectral documentations or commentaries. One could perhaps say that the text is one continuous long wandering with the photos as visual pauses. (The words of Elias Canetti suit this book by Sebald: "He didn't write his novels. He walked them.")

In America, Sebald has been acclaimed as a holocaust-writer on the level of Primo Levi. That seems to me to be an exaggeration, since holocaust does not function as a final explanation or as a starting-point or end-point. (Auschwitz is perhaps alluded to in the sound-association to Austerlitz and back to Aurach in *The Emigrants*). Theresienstadt is a reference to the holocaust, but the camp is not given any special novelistic status, and is only one example in a long parade of the *black boxes* of history, on the level of for instance the French National Library and the Belgian Palace of Justice; both being extensively scrutinised along the road without end that is the itinerary of the wanderer. The metaphor of the wanderer links the novel to Sebald's earlier book, *The Rings of Saturn*; in both cases we follow a discourse that is "wandering" in European history. The novel even "wanders" between European languages: it is of course written in German but makes an uninhibited use of English and French, sometimes even Flemish and Czech (the latter with translations).

This confusion of tongues contributes to the impression of the novel as a prosaic text: as one, single continuous text interfoliated by photos, which spectrally remind us of the reality of history. The strands of the text are contracted in a biographical narration: everything that the character Austerlitz searches for, finds and tells us about has to do with his life story, indirectly also with the Narrator's and therefore also with Sebald's own biography. This connection is emphasised by Sebald's "signing" of the text with ingenious arrangements contributing to the biographical touch of the text. I mentioned above that he gives his own pet-name as the first name of the painter Aurach in *The Emigrants*. "Max" returns on the final page of *Austerlitz*, now as one "Max Stern" that is said to be the name of a deported French jew, here given a date of disappearance that is also the birth date of Sebald himself.

I borrow another intricate example from the article "The Edge of Darkness" by Mark Anderson[21]: in the first story in *The Emigrants* we learn that Sebald's landlord has added to his emigration by changing his Jewish first name Hersch into the English Henry. That half-hidden "Hersch" comes back in the second story, now as "Hirsch" (deer): Sebald remembers that he had a "Hirschsprungspullover" as a school boy and that his teacher was drawing the deer on the black-board – a link that connects Sebald's own biography with Jewish *diaspora*. In *Austerlitz* the deer becomes French and is spelled "Cerf"; such is the name of the woman who is the landlady of Jacques Austerlitz in

21 Anderson 2003, p. 107.

Paris – at precisely the address where Paul Celan lived before taking his own life in 1970! These connections are allusions or secret patterns: Celan is never mentioned in *Austerlitz* but in this way he becomes, so to speak, written between the lines of the novel (and merges with the biographies of the title character and the narrator and Sebald) in ways that remind you of his own poetical versions of cryptic inscriptions. One suspects Sebald of elaborating any amount of textual net-work like this example; the result is that his texts become tightly knitted in at least two ways: by the biographical narrations and by these secretive inscriptions, giving the impression that "everything" is gathered in one, continuous text.

I now want to recall the fragment by Walter Benjamin quoted above on "prose" as the "universal-historical" text that is manifested in a messianic moment. Sebald certainly refrains from the messianic perspective but I still think that his ambition comes close to Benjamin's vision: I am now thinking of the emphatic multi-linguistic character of *Austerlitz*, of the thought-wanderings that make connections between any amount of different historical factors and phenomena, of the interconnection of biographical, historical and fictitious discourses and, not least, of the highly concentrated text, without spacing or chapters or sections, a tightening organisation that integrates all traces and emphasises coherence. Sebald's techniques for searching and remembering and reconstructing can all be regarded as efforts to find and construct coherence, to approach what Benjamin called the *integral prose* of universal history. As I have already said, I can find nothing of Benjamin's messianic suggestions in Sebald's project but I am still tempted to credit him with a claim for the universal. That is evident already in *Vertigo*, where he weaves stylised episodes from his own life into biographical anecdotes taken from the mythology of Stendhal and Kafka; in *The Emigrants*, where he identifies with the characters that are given a biography; in *The Rings of Saturn*, where he mixes with the perspectives and discourses of others; in *Austerlitz*, where he identifies his own searching with the research of the title character and, above all, makes it evident that the result of the research can only be more traces to follow and that the research therefore is without end. In the "universal history" that is glimpsed in the extension of this project *everything* is connected with everything; but since it is impossible to reach this finality one could just as well conclude that in the world of living history, *everything* is accidental and prey to the contingency of our existence.

It is precisely the effort to make the boundless amount of felicitous and cruel circumstances hang coherently and sensibly together that I associate with "prose", or at least with a prosaic tendency. When Sebald declares that *my medium is prose* I therefore regard it as more than trivial. It signals his project of *prosification* that is also an ambition of *aestheticisation*: to search for, construct, establish and perform an expressive and meaningful coherence. Ultimately this would result in a universal history where *everything* is connected with everything – balanced with the insight in the boundless contingency of everything that exists.

If I had to choose a single example to this tendency, it would have to be the ten pages long sentence in *Austerlitz*, where Sebald through Jacques Austerlitz describes Theresienstadt. The photos interfoliating these pages give a spectral reminder of past reality at the same time as making the whole sequence into a "dialectical image", to use Walter Benjamin's term. The reality that is reconstructed in this sentence was in itself a striking example of cruel contingency, dense coherence and hectic organisation (which is laconically commented on by the pictorial page reproducing a systematic disposition of the trades and activities of the camp). What the character Jacques Austerlitz looks for and tries to describe in this "image", and what the narrator Sebald reads through him and that we read through Sebald, is what "never was written". I am adopting the words of Hofmannsthal used by Benjamin in his determination of "prose" as referred to earlier in this essay. The term "prose" seems neutral, but is nevertheless an adequate naming of a project of integration, of a searching for meaningful coherence in what continues to be as meaningless as it is incomprehensible.

References:

Anderson, Mark 2003, "The Edge of Darkness." In: *October* 106 (2003).

Barthes, Roland 1986, "Rhetorical Analysis." In: *The Rustle of Language*. New York: Hill & Wang.

Benjamin, Walter 1991, *Der Begriff der Kunstkritik in der deutschen Romantik & Anmerkungen. Gesammelte Schriften* I :1 and I:3. Frankfurt: Suhrkamp.

Bürger, Peter 1988, *Prosa der Moderne*. Frankfurt: Suhrkamp.

Celan, Paul 1988, *Der Meridian und andere Prosa*. Frankfurt: Suhrkamp.

Dahlhaus, Carl 1982, *Musikalischer Realismus*. München: Piper.

Greene, Roland & Fowler, Elizabeth, ed. 1997, *The Project of Prose in early modern Europe and New World*. Cambridge University Press.

Hegel, G.W.F. 1970, *Vorlesungen über die Ästhetik. Werke* 14. Frankfurt: Suhrkamp.

Kittay, Jeffrey & Godzich, Wlad 1987, *The Emergence of Prose. An Essay in Prosaics*. Minnesota University Press.

Meschonnic, Henri 1982, *Critique du rythme. Anthropologie historique du langage*. Paris: Verdier.

Mullen, Harryette 2002, *Sleeping with the Dictionary*. University of California Press.

Nietzsche, Friedrich 1988, *Die fröhliche Wissenschaft*, *Kritische Studienausgabe* 3, Berlin: de Gruyter.

Sebald, W.G 2003, *Campo Santo*. München: Hanser. 2003 (1995), *Die Ringe des Saturn*. Frankfurt: Fischer. 2003 (2001), *Austerlitz*. Frankfurt: Fischer.

Shklovsky, Victor 1990, *Theory of Prose*. Transl. Benjamin Sher. Dalkey Archive press.

Todorov, Tzvetan 1971, *Poétique de la prose*. Paris: Seuil.